# Light
# ON LIFE'S
# Duties

D1002424

# Register This New Book

## Benefits of Registering*

- ✓ FREE **replacements** of lost or damaged books

- ✓ FREE **audiobook** – *Pilgrim's Progress*, audiobook edition

- ✓ FREE information about new titles and other **freebies**

www.anekopress.com/new-book-registration

*See our website for requirements and limitations.

# Light
# ON LIFE'S
# Duties

My Yoke Is Easy,
and My Burden Is Light

## F. B. MEYER

We love hearing from our readers. Please contact us at www.anekopress.com/questions-comments with any questions, comments, or suggestions.

*Cover Design: Jonathan Lewis*
*Editors: Donna Sundblad and Ruth Zetek*

Aneko Press

www.anekopress.com

Aneko Press, Life Sentence Publishing, and our logos are trademarks of

Life Sentence Publishing, Inc.
203 E. Birch Street
P.O. Box 652
Abbotsford, WI 54405

**RELIGION / Christian Life / Spiritual Growth**

Paperback ISBN: 978-1-62245-590-4

eBook ISBN: 978-1-62245-591-1

10  9  8  7  6  5  4  3  2

Available where books are sold

# Contents

# Foreword

After twelve years of ministry, a ministry that God was pleased to bless in many ways, I sat one day doing what a merchant would call "taking an account of stock." I could do nothing but praise the Lord for His goodness to me, but I found I was without what many others in whom I had perfect confidence claimed to have received. I experienced a feeling of unrest and a longing for God which never can be put into words. The darkness seemed to increase as the days passed. I felt I needed help from a source higher than man.

When I was ready to hear and obey, God spoke to me in a remarkable way. I was reading in a secular paper an extended account of the Northfield Conference, when my eyes lighted on the name of Reverend F. B. Meyer. I shall never forget one sentence of his: "If you are not willing to forsake all for Christ, then are you simply willing to say, 'I am willing to be made willing'?"

That was God's own message to my very soul, and Mr. Meyer brought it to me from Him. It was the crisis of my life. From that day on, I have read all that I could find coming from his pen.

I do not believe that there is a more intensely spiritual and, at the same time, so helpful and practical a writer in the world today as this man, whom I rejoice to call my friend.

These meditations are as sweet as honey in the honeycomb. They open up the deep things of God, but in such a helpful way that anyone can understand if he is only willing.

I could wish my friends no greater blessing than that Mr. Meyer's message might be to them all that it has been to me.

J. Wilbur Chapman
Albany, N.Y.

# Chapter 1

# In the King's House

The Christian experience can be compared to a suite of royal apartments, of which the first opens into the second, which again opens into the third, and so on. Of course, it's true that believers, since they are born into the royal, divine household, come into possession of it all. But, as a matter of fact, certain truths stand out more clearly to them at different stages of their spiritual journey, and as a result, their successive experiences can be compared to the chambers of a palace, through which they pass into the throne room and presence of their King.

The King Himself is waiting at the threshold to act as a guide. The key is in His hand, which opens, and no man shuts; which shuts, and no man opens (Revelation 3:7). Have you entered the first of those chambers? If not, He waits to unlock the first door to you, to all this at this moment, and to lead you forward from stage to stage, until you have realized everything that can be enjoyed by godly hearts on this side of the gates of pearl. Only be sure to follow where Jesus leads the way.

> *Draw me after thee, we will run.*
> (Song of Solomon 1:4)

### The First Chamber in the King's Holy Palace Is the Chamber of New Birth

The first chamber is preceded by a porch known as *Conviction for Sin*. But since the porch isn't part of the house, and we don't need to linger to describe it further.

Over the door of this chamber are inscribed the words: *Except a person be born again from above, . . . he cannot enter* (John 3:3, 5).

By nature, we are destitute of life – *dead in trespasses and sins* (Ephesians 2:1). For that reason, we don't need a new creed first, but a new life. The prophet's staff is good enough where there is life, but it's useless on the face of a dead babe (2 Kings 4:29-32). The first privilege is *life*. This is what the Holy Spirit gives us at the moment of conversion. He comes to us through some truth of the incorruptible Word of God and implants the first spark of the new life; and we who were dead, live. *And he has made you alive, who were dead in trespasses and sins* (Ephesians 2:1). Consequently, we enter the first room in our Father's palace, where the newborn babes are welcomed and nursed and fed.

**We don't need a new creed first, but a new life.**

We may remember the day and place of our new birth, or we may be as ignorant of them as we are of the circumstances of our natural birth. But what does it matter whether a person can recall his birthday or not, so long as he knows that he is alive?

In the same way an outstretched hand has two sides – the upper, called the back, and the under, called the palm – so there are two sides and names for the act of entrance into *The Chamber of New Birth*. Angels looking at it from the heaven side call it "being born again." Men, looking at it from the earth side call it "trusting Jesus." *Them that believe on his name* and *as many as received him, to them gave the power to become sons of God* (John 1:12). If you are born again, you will trust. And if you are trusting Jesus, however many your doubts and fears, you are certainly born again and have entered the palace. If you go no further, you will be saved, but you will miss countless blessings.

From the chamber of birth, where the newborn ones realize the throbbing of the life of God for the first time and rejoice together, there is a door that leads into a second chamber, which can be called *The Chamber of Assurance*.

Over that door, where the King awaits us with beckoning hand, these words are engraved: *Beloved, now we are the sons of God* (1 John 3:2). In many cases, of course, assurance follows immediately on conversion, like a father's kiss on his words of forgiveness to the contrite child. But it is also true that there are some truly saved souls who pass through weeks, months, and sometimes years without being sure of their standing in Jesus or deriving any comfort from it.

True assurance comes from the work of the Holy

Spirit through the sacred Scriptures. Read the Word and look for His teaching. Think ten times about Christ for every once you think about yourself. Think extensively on all the mentions of His finished work. Understand that you are so truly one with Him that you died in Him, laid with Him in the garden tomb, rose with Him, ascended with Him back to God, and have already been welcomed and accepted in the beloved. *Even as we were dead in sins, he has made us alive together with the Christ (by whose grace ye are saved) and has raised us up together and made us sit together in heavenly places in Christ Jesus* (Ephesians 2:5-6).

Remember that His Father is your Father, and that you are a son in the Son. As you live in these truths, opening your heart to the Holy Spirit, He will permeate your soul with a blessed conviction that you have eternal life and that you are a child – not because you feel it, but because God says so (John 3:36; Romans 8:16).

The door at the further end of this apartment leads into another chamber of the King. It is the door of consecration, leading into *The Chamber of a Surrendered Will.*

Above the doorway stand the words: *From now on let no one trouble me, for I bear in my body the marks of the Lord Jesus; whose I am and whom I serve* (Galatians 6:17; Acts 27:23). Consecration is giving Jesus His own. We are His by right because He bought us with His blood. Sadly, He hasn't received His money's worth. He paid for all but has had only a fragment of our energy, time, and earnings. By an act of consecration, let us ask Him to forgive the robbery of the past, and let us acknowledge our desire to be utterly and only for Him from this time forward – His slaves, His possessions, owning no master other than Him.

As soon as we say this, He will test our sincerity like He did the young ruler's in Luke 18:18-30, by asking something of us. He will lay His finger on something within us that He wants us to change – obeying some command or abstaining from some indulgence. If we instantly give up our will and way to Him, we pass through the narrow doorway into the chamber of surrender, which has a southern characteristic and is always warm and radiant with His presence, because obedience is the condition of manifested love. *Jesus answered and said unto him, He who loves me will keep my words, and my Father will love him, and we will come unto him and dwell with him* (John 14:23).

This doorway is very narrow, and the entrance is only possible for those who lay aside weights as well as sins. A weight is anything which, without being essentially wrong or hurtful to others, is still a hindrance to us. We can always identify a weight by three signs: first, we are uneasy about it; second, we argue for it against our conscience; and third, we go about asking people's advice as to whether or not we can continue it without harm. All these things must be laid aside in the strength which Jesus waits to give. Ask Him to deal with them for you, so you can be ready and act together *in every good work to do his will* (Hebrews 13:21).

At the further end of this apartment, another door invites us to enter *The Chamber of the Filling of the Spirit*. Above the entrance glistens the words: *Be filled with the Spirit* (Ephesians 5:18). We gladly admit that the Holy Spirit is literally in the heart of every true believer, *the Spirit of God dwells in you* (Romans 8:9), and that the whole work of grace in our souls is due to Him, from the first desire to be saved to the last prayer breathed on the threshold of heaven. But it is also true that a time comes in our education when we become more easily impressed regarding the necessity of the Holy Spirit and seek for more of His all-pervading, heart-filling presence.

Many of us have been startled to discover we've been content with too little of the Holy Spirit. There has been enough throne water to cover the stones in the riverbed but not to fill its channel. Instead of occupying all, our gracious Guest has been confined to one or two back rooms of our heart, in the same way a poor housekeeper sometimes dwells in the attic or the cellar to keep a mansion, while the suites of splendid apartments are consigned to layers of dust and cobwebs, shuttered, dismantled, and locked.

Each Christian has the Holy Spirit, but each Christian needs more and more of Him until the whole nature is filled. Rather, it would be truer to say the Holy Spirit wants more and more of us. Let us ask our heavenly Father to give us of His Spirit in always increasing measures, and as we ask, let us yield ourselves continually to His indwelling and inworking. Then let us believe we are filled, not because we *feel* it, but because we are sure God is keeping His Word to us: *Ye shall not see wind, neither shall ye see rain; yet this valley shall be filled with water* (2 Kings 3:17).

It is true that the filling of the Spirit involves a

separation, a giving up, a living apart, which is keenly bitter to the flesh. The filling of Pentecost is a baptism of fire, but the Son of God walks beside us amid the flames where there is joy as the bonds shrivel and limbs are freed.

But this chamber leads to another of surpassing blessedness, *The Chamber of Abiding in Christ.* Around the doorway a vine is sculptured with trailing branches and dangling grapes; and intertwined among the foliage, these words appear: *Abide in me, and I in you. As the branch cannot bear fruit of itself, except it abides in the vine, no more can ye, except ye abide in me* (John 15:4). The Holy Spirit never reveals Himself. Those who have most of His grace, "think it not." His chosen work is to reveal the Lord. We are not necessarily conscious of the Spirit, but of Him who is the Alpha and the Omega of our life. *I AM the Alpha and the Omega, beginning and end, saith the Lord, who is and who was and who is to come, the Almighty* (Revelation 1:8). Where the Spirit is in full possession, Christ's loveliness fills the soul like the scent of the ointment filled the house at Bethany.

Our Lord is with us every day, but often our eyes assert that we don't know Him, and if we discern Him for a radiant moment, He vanishes from our sight. However, there are times when we not only *believe* He is near, but we also *perceive* His presence by the instinct of the heart. He becomes a living, bright reality, sitting over our hearth, walking beside us through the crowded streets, sailing with us across the stormy lake, standing beside the graves that hold our dead, sharing our crosses and our burdens, turning the water of common joys into the wine of holy sacraments. Then the believer leans hard on the ever-present Lord, drawing on His fullness, appropriating His unsearchable riches, and claiming His grace to turn every temptation into ways of increasing our likeness to Himself. And if the branch abides constantly in the Vine, it can't help bearing fruit. No, the difficulty would be to keep the fruit back. *I AM the vine, ye are the branches: he that abides in me, and I in him, the same brings forth much fruit; for without me ye can do nothing* (John 15:5).

We have to do with the death and not with the life part of our experience. *For if ye live according to the flesh, ye shall die; but if through the Spirit ye mortify the deeds of the body, ye shall live* (Romans 8:13). The more often we sow ourselves in the clods of daily self-denial, falling into the furrows to die, the more fruit we bear. It is by *always bearing about in the body the dying of the Lord Jesus, that the life also of Jesus might be made manifest in our body* (2 Corinthians 4:10). Prune off every bud on the old stock, and all the energy will pass up to the rare flowers and fruits grafted there by heaven.

But see the King summoning us forward into *The Chamber of Victory over Sin*. Above the door are the words: *Whosoever abides in him does not sin* (1 John 3:6). Around the walls hang various instruments of war: *Therefore, take unto you the whole armour of God, that ye may be able to withstand in the evil day and stand fast, all the work having been finished* (Ephesians 6:13), and murals of the overcomers receiving the just rewards which the King has promised. *He that overcomes I will make a pillar in the temple of my God, and he shall go out no more, and I will write upon him the name of my God, and the name of the city of my God which is the new Jerusalem, which comes down out of heaven from and with my God, and I will write upon him my new name* (Revelation 3:12). We must be careful of the order in which we put these things. Many seek victory over sin before yielding themselves entirely to God. But you can never enter this chamber where the palm branch waves unless you have passed through the chamber of consecration. Give yourself up entirely to Jesus, and He will keep you.

Will you dare to say that He can hold the oceans in the hollow of His hand, and sustain the arch of heaven, and fill the sun with light for millenniums, but that He can't keep you from being overcome by sin or filled with the impulsive rush of unholy passion? Can He not deliver His saints from the sword, His children from the power of those outside the church? Is all power given Him in heaven and on earth, and yet He must stand paralyzed before the devils that possess you, unable to cast them out? To ask such questions is to answer them. *I know whom I have believed and am persuaded that he is able to keep* (2 Timothy 1:12).

We can expect to be tempted until we die, and we will certainly carry with us an evil nature, which could manifest itself, unless it is kept in check by the grace of God. But if we abide in Christ, and He abides in us – if we live under the power of the Holy Spirit – temptation won't excite any fascination in us. On the contrary, it shall horrify us with the least stirring of our self-life instantly noticed and met by the name and blood and

Spirit of Jesus. The tides of His purity and life will flow so strongly over our being that they will sweep away any black drops of ink oozing upward from the sands.

In spite of this, you must once and for all shut the back door as well as the front door against sin. You must make every effort not to linger with it in any form. You must see that by the purpose of God you are limited to godliness. *For unto those whom he knew beforehand, he also marked out beforehand the way that they might be conformed to the image of his Son, that he might be the firstborn among many brethren* (Romans 8:29). You must definitely and forever opt for the cross as the destiny of your self-life, and you will find that He will save you from all that you dare to trust Him with. *Every place that the sole of your foot shall tread upon, that have I given unto you* (Joshua 1:3). And His work within us is most perfect when it is least apparent, and when the flesh is kept so completely in check that we begin to think it has been altogether extracted.

> You must definitely and forever opt for the cross as the destiny of your self-life.

Yet another door at the far end of this chamber summons us to come forward to *The Chamber of Heart Rest.*

The King Himself spoke this motto in Matthew 11:29: *Take my yoke . . . and ye shall find rest for your souls.* Soft notes of a tune float on the air; the peace of God stands sentry against intruding care. Of course, the soul learns something about rest at the very beginning, but these words of the Master indicate there are at least two kinds of rest. And so, the rest of forgiveness passes into the rest of surrender and satisfaction.

We lay our worries and cares where once we only laid our sins. We lose the unrestrained fever and swiftness of earlier days and become oblivious to praise on the one hand and censure on the other. Our soul is poised on God, satisfied with God, and seeks nothing outside of God. It regards all things from the standpoint of eternity and of God. The life loses the senseless babble of its earlier course and sweeps onward to the ocean from which it derived its life, with a stillness which speaks of its depth and a serenity which foretells its destiny. The very face communicates the tale of the sweet, still life within, which is in harmony with the everlasting chime of the land where storms, conflict, and alarm do not come.

Some say that the door at the end of this chamber leads into *The Chamber of Fellowship in Christ's Sufferings*, and that may be so. All along the Christian's course there is a great and growing love for the world for which He died. But there are times when that love feels more like an agony of compassion and desire; and there are sufferings caused by the thorn-crown, including the sneer, the mockery, the cross, the spear, and the baptism of blood and tears. All these fall to the portion of the followers of the King, and possibly they come most plentifully to the godliest who are most like the Lord. But it is certain that those who suffer in this way are those who reign. Their sufferings aren't for a moment to be compared to the glory revealed in their lives. And out of their bitter griefs, sweetened by the cross, gush springs of water to refresh the weary inheritance of God, like the waters of Exodus. *And when they came to Marah, they could not drink of the waters of Marah, for they were bitter; therefore the name of it was called Marah. Then the people murmured against Moses, saying, What shall we drink? And he cried unto the LORD; and the LORD showed him a tree, which when he had cast it into the waters, the waters were made sweet* (Exodus 15:23-25).

Beyond all these – separated from them by a very slight distance – are *The Mansions of the Father's House* into which the King will soon lead us, with chamber after chamber of delight, and stretch after stretch of golden glory, until these natures of ours, which are only like an infant's, have developed to the measure of the stature of our full growth into the likeness of the Son of God.

O soul! Where have you gone to? Don't linger inside the first chamber but press onward making forward progress. If any door seems locked, knock, and it shall be opened unto you. *Ask, and it shall be given you; seek, and ye shall find; knock, and it shall be opened unto you* (Matthew 7:7). Never think you've already achieved the goal or are already perfect, but follow onward to apprehend all for which Jesus Christ apprehended you. *Press toward the mark for the prize of the high calling of God in Christ Jesus* (Philippians 3:14).

## Chapter 2

# The Lost Chord

The story of "The Lost Chord" has been told in exquisite verse and stately music. We have all heard about the lady who laid her fingers on the open keys of a glorious organ as the autumn twilight softly filled the room. She didn't know what she was playing, or what she was dreaming then, but she struck one chord of music, like the sound of a great amen.

> It flooded the crimson twilight,
>     Like the close of an angel's psalm,
> And it lay on my fevered spirit
>     With the touch of infinite calm:
>
> It quieted pain and sorrow,
>     Like love overcoming strife;
> It seemed the harmonious echo
>     From our discordant life.

> It linked all perplexed meanings
> Into one perfect peace,
> And trembled away into silence,
> As if it were loth to cease.[1]

Something called her away, and when she returned to the organ, she had lost that divine chord. Though she longed for it, and sought it, it was all in vain. It was a lost chord.

Whenever I hear that story, it reminds me of the lost joy, the lost peace, the lost power so many complain about. At the beginning of their Christian life, or recently, or further in the past, it seemed as if they had struck the chord of a blessed and glorious life. As long as those notes lingered in their lives, they were like days of heaven on earth; but sadly, those notes soon died away into silence, and all their life is now filled with regret for the grace of days that are dead.

> Where is the blessedness I knew
> When first I sought the Lord?
> Where is the soul-refreshing view
> Of Jesus and His Word?
>
> What peaceful hours I then enjoyed!
> How sweet their memory still!
> But they have left an aching void
> The world can never fill.[2]

These words are written to help all such people and to give them the sweet lost chord again. Take heart! You

---

1    "The Lost Chord," by Adelaide A. Procter

2    William Cowper, "O For a Closer Walk with God," *Conyer's Collection of Psalms and Hymns*, 1772.

can have it all again and more than all you ever lost. You have flung your precious stones into the deep; for a moment they created a splash, followed by a tiny ripple, and then the stones sunk down, apparently beyond hope of recovery. Yet the hand of Christ will again place them on your palm. Only in the future, be wise enough to let Him keep them for you.

These are the steps back you can take at once:

### 1. Be Certain God Will Give You a Hearty Welcome

God's portrait is drawn by One who couldn't mislead us, who compares Him to the Father of a loved prodigal son, always watching the road from His windows, and eagerly longing for his return. If He should see him a great way off, He is ready to run to meet him, and embrace him to His yearning heart – rags, filth, and all.

That is your God, my friend. Listen to His words, broken by laments: *How must I leave thee, Ephraim? how shall I give thee up, Israel? how could I make thee as Admah? nor set thee as Zeboim? my heart churns within me; all my compassion is inflamed* (Hosea 11:8). Read the last chapter of the book of Hosea. This chapter may well be called the backsliders' gospel.

Read the third chapter of Jeremiah, and let the sorrowful pleadings return to soak into your spirit. Read the story of Peter's fall and restoration, and let your tears fall thick and fast on John 21 as you learn how gracefully the Lord forgave, and how generously He entrusted the backslider with His sheep and His lambs. Be certain that even though your repeated failures and sins have worn out everyone else, they have not exhausted the infinite love of God. He tells us to forgive our offending brother to four hundred and ninety times. Won't He forgive us much more often? As high as the heavens are above the earth, so great is His mercy. *Let the wicked forsake his way, and the unrighteous man his thoughts: and let him return unto the LORD, and he will have mercy upon him; and to our God, for he will abundantly pardon* (Isaiah 55:7). If you go back to God, you are sure of a hearty welcome.

## 2. Seek to Know and Confess Whatever Has Come between God and You

You may have lost the light of God's face, not because He has arbitrarily withdrawn it, but because your sins have come between you and your God. Like a cloud before the sun, your sins may have hidden His face from you. As God if this is so, and be honest with yourself if you already know this to be true. Don't spend time looking at them as a whole. Deal with them one by one. The Boer[3] is a formidable foe to the British soldier because he is trained from boyhood to take definite aim and bring down his mark, while our soldiers fire in volleys. In dealing with sin, we should imitate the Boer in the certainty and accuracy of his aim.

Ask God to search you and show you what wicked way is in you. Put all your life in order before Him – in

---

3    The term *Boer* is derived from the Afrikaans word for "farmer" and was used to describe the people in southern Africa who traced their ancestry to Dutch, German, and French Huguenot settlers. The South African Boer War between the British Empire and the Boers lasted from 1899-1902.

the same way Joshua sorted through Israel – and sift through it, tribe by tribe, family by family, household by household, man by man, until you finally find the Achan who has robbed you of the blessed smile of God. Don't say, "Lord, I'm a great sinner, I've done what I shouldn't, and I haven't done what I should." Instead, say, "Lord, I have sinned in this, and this, and that, and the other." Be specific. Call up each sin by its right name to receive the sentence of death. Your heart is choked with sins; empty it out like you would a box, by first

> Never rest until all [sins] are gone.

dealing with the articles that lie on the surface. When you have removed them, you will see more underneath; deal with them also. When these are removed, you will probably see some more. Never rest until all are gone. This is the process of confession – this process of telling God the unvarnished story – the sad, sad story of each accursed sin: how it began, how you sinfully permitted it to grow, how you have loved and followed it to your bitter cost.

### 3. Believe in God's Instant Forgiveness

How long does it take you to forgive your child when you are sure they are really sorry and repentant? Not a moment. Time isn't considered in forgiveness. The estrangement of a lifetime, the wrongdoing of years, can be forgiven in the twinkling of an eye – in the time it takes for a tear to form and fall. That is how it is with God. *If we confess our sins, he is faithful and just to forgive us* (1 John 1:9).

Sometimes He keeps us waiting for an answer to other prayers, but He never keeps us waiting one single second for an answer to our prayer for forgiveness. It is hardly possible for the prodigal to stammer out the words, "Father, I have sinned," before the answer flashes upon him: "I have put away thy sin; thou shalt not die" (2 Samuel 12:13). There isn't a moment's interlude between the humble and sad telling of the story of sin and God's forgiveness. As soon as a repentant person appears in the doorway of God's throne room, the golden scepter of His royal forgiveness is stretched out for him to touch. You might not *feel* forgiven, and you may have no joyful ecstasy, but in God's thinking, you are forgiven. The angels hear Him say, "Child, your sins, which are many, are all forgiven. Go in peace." *Therefore I say unto thee, Her sins, which are many, are forgiven; for she loved much; but to whom little is forgiven, the same loves little* (Luke 7:47).

If we confess, and as soon as we confess, He is faithful and just to forgive. He never says, "Go your way and return tomorrow, and I will see whether I can forgive." He hates the sin and is only too glad to sweep it away. He loves the sinner and is only too happy to receive him again in His embrace. And He is able to do all this so quickly and so completely because Jesus Christ our Lord bore our sins in His own body on the tree. *He himself bore our sins in his own body on the tree, that we, being dead to sins, should live unto righteousness* (1 Peter 2:24).

### 4. Give Up the Cause of Past Failure

True repentance shows itself eager not to offend again. This care prompts the sinner to go back to consider his past life to discover how he came to sin and to avoid that cause.

Is it a friendship? Then he will cut the tender cord even if it's the thread of his life.

Is it an amusement? Then he will forever stay away from that place, those settings, and that companionship.

Is it a profitable means of making money? Then he would rather live on a crust of bread than follow it a moment longer.

Is it a study, a pursuit, a book? Then he would rather lose a hand, or a foot, or an eye, than miss the favor of God, which is life. *And if thy right hand should bring thee occasion to stumble, cut it off, and cast it from thee: for it is better for thee that one of thy members should perish, and not that thy whole body should be cast into hell* (Matthew 5:30).

Is it something that the church permits? Nevertheless, to him it shall be sin.

If you can't walk on ice without slipping or falling, it is better not to go on it at all. If you can't digest certain food, it is better not to put it into your mouth. It might seem impossible to disentangle yourself from certain entanglements which have woven themselves around you; nevertheless, remember Him who said, *Let my people go, that they may serve me* again and again in the book of Exodus. He cut the knot of bondage for them, and if you trust Him, He will cut it for you. Or if He doesn't cut it with a single blow, He will untie it by the patient workings of His foresight and wisdom.

### 5. Take Any Public Step That May Be Necessary

It isn't enough to confess to God; if you have sinned against another person, you must also confess to him. *Leave thy gift there before the altar, and go; first restore friendship with thy brother* (Matthew 5:24). If you have done him a wrong, go and tell him so. If you have defrauded him, whether he knows it or not, send him the amount you have taken or kept back and add to it something to compensate for his loss. Under the Levitical law, it was decreed that the delinquent person should restore what he took away violently or by falsehood, and should add one-fifth part to it, and only then might he come with his trespass offering to the priest and be forgiven. This principle still holds true today. You will never be happy until you have made restitution. Write the letter or make the call at once. And if the one whom you defrauded is no longer alive, then make the debt right with his heirs and representatives. You must roll away this stone from the grave, or the dead joy can never arise, however loudly you may call it to come forth. I don't believe in a repentance that isn't honorable enough to make amends for the past, in whatever manner is within your reach.

### 6. Give Your Whole Heart Once and Forever to God

You may have given your heart to God before, but do it again. You may never have done it, and if that's the case, then do it for the first time. Kneel down and give yourself, your life, your interests, your all, to God. Lay the sacrifice on the altar. If you can't *give*, then ask God to come and *take*. Tell Him that you wish to be only, always, and totally for Him. We might well hesitate to give the glorious Lord such a handful of withered leaves if He hadn't expressly asked us each to give Him our heart. *My son, give me thine heart, and let thine eyes observe my ways* (Proverbs 23:26). It is very wonderful, but He wouldn't make such a request if He didn't really mean it. No doubt, He can make something out of our poor nature: a vessel for His use, a weapon for His hand, a receptacle for His glory, a crown for His brow.

> Give yourself, your life, your interests, your all, to God.

### 7.  Trust God to Keep You in All the Future

The old version of the Bible used to tell us that He was able to keep us from *falling*. The new version, giving a closer rendering of the Greek, tells us that He is able to guard us from *stumbling*. He can and so He will. But we must trust Him. Moment by moment we must look into His face and say, *Keep me as the apple of the eye; hide me with the shadow of thy wings* (Psalm 17:8). He will never fail you. He will never fail you nor forsake you. He will give His angels charge to keep you in all your ways. He will cover you with His feathers, and under His wings you will have confidence (Psalm 91:4, 11).

But you say, "I fail to look into His face at the moment of temptation." If that's the case, then do this: ask the

Holy Spirit, whose responsibility it is to bring all things to our remembrance, to remind you to look to Jesus when you are in danger. Each morning, entrust yourself into His hands. Look to Him to help keep you looking toward Him. Trust in Him to keep you trusting. Don't look at your difficulties or weaknesses, and don't keep thinking you will fall again someday. Go through life, whispering, saying, singing a thousand times a day, "Jesus saves me now."[4]

A friend once told me that she had been kept from backsliding in this way: in the presence of God, she took time each night to consider quietly where she had lost ground during the day, and if she felt she had done so, she never slept until she had asked to be forgiven and restored.

This practice is also good and beneficial for you and me, dear reader. So, let us repair the little crack within the lute, for fear that over time it might spread and make our music mute, and slowly widen to silence the music altogether.

If these directions are followed, the lost chord will no longer be lost, nor will we have to wait until God's great angel sounds it, because it will ring again in our heart and make sweet music in our life.

---

4    A. C. Downer, "Jesus Saves Me Now," *Christian Hymns No. 1* (1899), 179.

# Chapter 3

# Victory over Sin

The longer I live and learn about the experiences of most Christian people, the more I long to hear them, because they unfold glimpses of that life of peace, power, and victory over sin, which our heavenly Father has made possible for us. Blessed secrets in the Bible are hidden from the wise and prudent but are revealed to babes, and once these are understood and accepted, they will wipe away many a tear and shed sunshine on many a darkened pathway. *That which eye has not seen nor ear heard neither has entered into the heart of man is that which God has prepared for those that love him* (1 Corinthians 2:9).

The bitterest experience with most believers is the presence and power of sin. They long to walk through this grimy world with pure hearts and stainless garments, but while they desire to do good, evil is present within them. They consent to God's law – that it is good; they approve it; they even delight in it according to the inward man. They do their best to keep it; but, even so, they seem as helpless to perform it as a person with a brain struck with paralysis is helpless to walk straight. Rivers of salty tears have fallen on the open pages of the Penitent's Psalm (Psalm 51), shed by those who could repeat every word of it by heart. And regiments of weary feet have walked the Bridge of Sighs (Romans 7), which vividly sets forth the experience of a person who hasn't learned God's secret.

Surely, our God must have provided for all this. It wouldn't have been like Him to fill us with hatred toward sin and longings for holiness if there were no escape from the tyranny of the one, and no possibility of attaining the other. To save us from sinning on the other side of the pearly gates would be a small matter, but we want to be saved from sinning now in this dark world. In fact, we want it for the sake of the world so it can be involved attracted and convinced. We want it for our own peace, which can't be perfected while we groan under a bondage worse than the Egyptian's. We want it for the glory of God, which would then be reflected from us, with undimming brightness, like sunshine from burnished metal.

### What Does the Word of God Lead Us to Expect?

Before Abraham arose to walk the length and breadth of the Land of Promise, God told Him to *lift up now thine eyes and look* (Genesis 13:14). And before we can enter into the enjoyment of our privileges in Jesus Christ, we must know what they are – something of their length and breadth, and depth and height.

### 1. We Must Not Expect to Be Free from Temptation

Our *adversary the devil, as a roaring lion, walks about, seeking whom he may devour* (1 Peter 5:8). He tempted our Lord, and he will tempt us. He will entice us to do wrong using every avenue of sense, pouring his evil suggestions through eye, ear, touch, mouth, and mind. If he doesn't attack us himself, he can set any one of his countless agents on us. They will softly step behind us and quietly suggest many serious blasphemies, which we will think proceeded from our own mind.

But temptation isn't necessarily sin. A man may ask me to share the spoils of a burglary, but if I indignantly refuse and keep my doors shut tight against him, no one can accuse me of receiving stolen property. Our Lord was tempted in all the ways we are, yet without sin. You might go through hell itself, abounding with all manner of awful suggestions, and still not sin. God wouldn't allow Satan to tempt us if temptation automatically led to sin, but temptation doesn't do so. As long as the will refuses to comply with the solicitation or strike at the bait, there is no sin.

Temptation may even be a blessing to a person when it reveals his weakness to him and drives him to the almighty Savior. Don't be surprised, then, dear child of God, if you are tempted at every step of your earthly journey, and almost beyond what you can endure. You won't *be tempted above what ye are able but will with the temptation also make a way to escape* (1 Corinthians 10:13).

## 2. We Must Not Expect to Lose Our Sinful Nature

When we are born again, a new life – the life of God – is put into us by the Holy Spirit. But the old self-life, which in Scripture is called *the flesh*, is not taken away. The two can coexist in the same heart. *For the flesh lusts against the Spirit, and the Spirit against the flesh* (Galatians 5:17). The presence of this old self-life within our heart can be detected by its rising up, upsetting us, wearing us down, and moving us toward sin, when temptation calls to it from outside. It can seem as still as death when facing the increasing power of the new life is noticeable, but that old nature is still present in the depths of our makeup, like a Samson in the dark dungeons of Philistia. The possibility and a fear of its strength growing again to our shame and hurt is always there.

> Don't ignore the presence of a sinful nature within you, with its tendencies and possibilities for sin.

Don't ignore the presence of a sinful nature within you, with its tendencies and possibilities for sin. Many people have been deceived into neglect and ignorance by the idea that the root of sin had been plucked from their heart, and that for this reason they wouldn't sin again. Then, in the face of some sudden uprising of their old nature, they are filled with agony and shame, even if they haven't dropped back into a sea of ink for a moment. *If we say that we have no sin, we deceive ourselves, and there is no truth in us* (1 John 1:8).

There is a difference between *sin* and *sins*. *Sin* is the root-principle of evil, *the flesh*, the old self-life, the

26

bias and tendency to sin, which can be kept in check by the grace of God, but which remains in us, though in diminishing power, until we leave this world. *Sins* are the outcome of this – manifestations in act of the sinful nature within. Through the grace of Jesus, we can be saved from these daily. *And she shall bring forth a son, and thou shalt call his name Jesus, for he shall save his people from their sins* (Matthew 1:21). To put the matter clearly, *sin* isn't dead in us, but we can be dead *to sin* so it won't bear the deadly fruits of *sins*.

### 3. We Must Not Expect to Be Free from Liability to Sin

What is sin? It is the "Yes" of the will to temptation. It is very difficult to express the delicate workings of our heart, but when we are tempted, doesn't something like this happen to us? A temptation is presented to us suddenly and makes a strong appeal. This can immediately cause a quavering movement of the old nature, like the way strings of a violin or piano vibrate in answer to sounds exciting the air. Some don't feel this tremulous response; others do, though I believe it will get fainter and fainter as believers treat it with continued neglect, so that finally, in the matured saint, it will become almost imperceptible. This response indicates the presence of the evil nature within, which is in itself hateful in the sight of our Holy God, and should be regretted and confessed and always needs the presence of the blood of Jesus to counteract and atone; but that tremulous movement hasn't as yet developed into an actual overt sin for which we are responsible and for which we need to repent.

Sin is the act of the will and is only possible when the will agrees to some unholy influence. The tempter presenting his temptation through the senses and emotions makes an appeal to the will, which is our real self. If that will instantly shudders, like chickens when the hawk hovers in the sky above them, and cries, "How can I do this great wickedness and sin against God?" and immediately looks to Jesus, then there are, so far as I understand, no sins. If, on the other hand, the will begins to trifle with temptation, to linger with it, and to yield to it, then we have stepped out of the light into the dark. We have broken God's law, splashed our white robes, and brought ourselves into condemnation. We are accountable for this as long as we are in this world, for we can live a godly, righteous, sober life for years; but if we look away from God for only a moment, our will can suddenly be mastered, in the same way Louis XVIII was mastered by the mob that invaded his palace. And, like David, we can be hurried into a sin which will destroy our peace and blacken our character for the future.

Now, what are the secrets of victory over sin?

## 1. Remember That the Blood of Jesus Is Always at Work Cleansing You

It is sweet to notice the present tenses of Scripture in Psalm 103:3-6. The Lord forgives, heals, redeems, crowns, satisfies, and executes righteousness and justice. But the sweetest of all is *the blood of Jesus Christ,*

*... cleanses us from all sin* (1 John 1:7). It cleansed us when we first knelt at His cross. It will clean away the last remnant of sin as we cross the golden threshold. But it *does* cleanse us every hour, in the same way the brook flows over the stones in its bed until they glisten with lustrous beauty, and like the tear constantly cascades over the eye, and keeps it bright and clean, in spite of all the filth that darkens the air.

Having a sinful nature is an evil that always needs an antidote. The risings and stirrings of that nature under the enticement of temptation always need cleansing. The permission of things we now count harmless in our life we will someday condemn and put away in the midst of increasing light – all these need forgiveness. But for all these needs, there is more than enough provision for us in the blood of Jesus, which is always crying to God for us. Even when we don't plead it or remember it, or realize our need of it, it accomplishes for us and in us its unceasing ministry of blessing.

## 2. Reckon Yourself Dead to the Appeals of Sin

Sin has no power over a dead man. Dress it in its most bewitching guise, and it still doesn't cause him to stir. Tears and smiles and words and blows all fail to awaken a response from that cold corpse. No plea will stir it until it hears the voice of the Son of God.

This is our position with respect to the appeals of sin. God looks on us as having been crucified with Christ and being dead with Him. *I am crucified with Christ; nevertheless I live; yet not I, but Christ lives in me, and the life which I now live in the flesh I live by the faith of the Son of God, who loved me and gave himself for me* (Galatians 2:20). In Him, we have passed out of the world of sin and death and into the world of resurrection glory. This is our position in the mind of God, and it is for us to take it up and make it real by faith. We might not *feel* any big difference, but we must *believe* there is and act as if there is. Our children sometimes play at make-believe; we too are to make believe, and when we do, we will soon come to feel as we believe. Then, when a temptation solicits you, say, "I am dead to you. Don't spend your energies on one who is oblivious to your spells and callous to your charms. You have no more power over me than over my Lord and Head." *Likewise also reckon yourselves to be truly dead unto sin, but alive unto God in Christ, Jesus, our Lord* (Romans 6:11).

### 3. Walk in the Spirit; Keep in Step with the Holy Spirit

The Holy Spirit is in the heart of every believer. *But ye are not in the flesh, but in the Spirit, because the Spirit of God dwells in you. Now if anyone does not have the Spirit of Christ, that person is not of him* (Romans 8:9). But sadly, too often He is shut up in some meager attic in the back of the house, while the world fills the rest. As long as it is like this, there's one long, weary story of defeat and unrest. But He is not content. *Do ye think that the scripture says in vain, The spirit that dwells in us lusts to envy?* (James 4:5). Those who yield to Him are happy. He will fill them like the tide fills the harbor and lifts the barges off the banks of mud. He will live in them, extensively shedding the perfume of the love of Jesus and will reveal the deep things of God.

With the Spirit of God, we can always tell when we are wrong. Our conscience darkens in a moment when we have grieved Him. If we are aware of such a darkness, it is best never to rest until we have discovered the cause revealed by His electrifying light, and confessed it and put it away.

Besides this, if we live and walk in the Spirit, we will find that He will work against the risings of our old nature, counteracting them in the same way disinfecting power counteracts the germs of disease floating in an infected house, *so that ye cannot do the things that ye would* (Galatians 5:17). These are some of the most precious words in the New Testament. If you have never tried it, I implore you to begin to test it in your daily life. *Walk in the Spirit* hour by hour, through vigilant obedience to His slightest promptings, and you will find that *ye shall not fulfil the lust of the flesh* (Galatians 5:16).

## 4. As Soon as You Are Aware of Temptation, Look Instantly to Jesus

Flee to Him quicker than a chicken runs beneath the shelter of its mother's wing when the falcon is in the air. In the morning, before you leave your room, commit yourself definitely into His hands, confident that *he is able to keep that which I have committed unto him* (2 Timothy 1:12). Go from your room with the assurance that He will cover you with His feathers and from under His wings you will trust. And when the tempter comes, look instantly up and say, "Jesus, I am trusting Thee to *keep* me."[5]

This is what the apostle Paul calls using the shield of faith. The upward glance of faith puts Jesus like a shield between the tempter and yourself. You can go through life saying a hundred times a day, "Jesus saves me," and He will never let those who trust in Him be ashamed. He *is powerful to keep you without sin and to present you faultless before the presence of his glory with exceeding joy* (Jude 24). You can be pressed with temptations externally, and may feel the workings of evil within, and yet as your will looks intently to Jesus, you will remain steadfast, immovable, and unyielding. No weapon that is forged against you in the armory of hell will prosper.

## 5. There Is Something Better Even than This

I was first taught this by a gray-haired clergyman, in the study of the Deanery, at Southampton. Once, when tempted to feel great irritation, he told us that he looked up and claimed the patience and gentleness of Christ. Since then, it had become the practice of his life to claim from Him the virtue which he felt deficient in himself. In times of unrest, "Your peace, Lord." In times of irritation, "Your patience, Lord." In times of temptation, "Your purity, Lord." In times of weakness, "Your strength, Lord." For me, it was a message straight from the throne. Until that time, I'd been content with ridding myself of burdens. Now I began to reach out

---

5    Frances R. Havergal, "I Am Trusting Thee, Lord Jesus," *Lutheran Hymnal*, 1874.

in view of a positive blessing, making each temptation the opportunity for the new acquisition of gold leaf. Try it, dear reader.

When I have spoken in this way in public, I have been met at times by the objection, "Ah, sir, it is quite true that the Lord will keep me if I look to Him, but I often forget to look in time." This arises from one of three causes.

*Perhaps the heart and life have never been entirely surrendered to Jesus.* Constant defeat always indicates a failure in consecration. You must not expect Christ to keep you unless you have given your heart and life entirely over to Him, so that He is king. Christ can't be keeper if He is not king. And He will not be king at all unless He is king of all.

> Christ can't be keeper if He is not king.

*Or perhaps there is a lack of watchfulness.* Christ will not keep us if we carelessly and shamelessly put ourselves into the path of temptation. He will give His angels charge over us in every path of duty, but not to catch us every time we like to throw ourselves from the jutting height. *Watch and pray, that ye enter not into temptation* (Matthew 26:41).

*Or perhaps there is a lack of feeding on the Word of God.* No one can live a life of faith without times of prolonged waiting on God in the loving study of the Bible and in prayer. The man who doesn't make time for private devotions in the early morning can hardly expect to walk with God all day. And of the two things, the devout meditation on the Word is more important to soul-health than even prayer. It is more necessary for you to hear God's words than it is for God to hear yours, although the one will always lead to the other. Focus on these things and it will become both easy and natural to trust Christ in the time of afflictions or temptations.

If, despite all these helps, you are still deceived into a sin and overtaken by a weakness, don't lose heart. If a sheep and a sow fall into a ditch, the sow wallows in it, but the sheep bleats pathetically until she is cleansed by her master. Go at once to your compassionate Savior. Tell Him in the simplest words the story of your fall and the sorrow you feel. Ask Him to wash you at once and to restore your soul, and, while you are asking, believe that it is done. Then go to anyone against or with whom you have sinned, and *confess your faults one to another* (James 5:16). In this way, the *peace of God, which passes all understanding, shall keep your hearts and minds through Christ Jesus* (Philippians 4:7), and will return to roost in your heart and to guard it like a sentry-angel in shining armor.

And if you live in this way, free from the power of sin, you will find that the Master will begin to use you as never before and to tell you His heart-secrets and to open to you the royal magnificence of a life hidden with Himself in God.

May this be your happy portion, dear reader.

## Chapter 4

# Stepping into the Blessed Life

There is a Christian life, which, in comparison with what is experienced by the majority of Christians, is as different as summer is to winter or as the mature fruitfulness of a golden autumn is to the struggling promise of a cold and late spring. Caleb might have lived such a life in Hebron, the city of fellowship, or as the apostle John lived when he wrote his epistles. It might properly be called the blessed life.

The blessedness of the blessed life lies in this: that we trust the Lord to do in us and for us what we cannot do ourselves. In doing so, we find that He does not contradict His Word, but that, *according to your faith be it unto you* (Matthew 9:29). The weary spirit that has unsuccessfully sought to realize its ideal by its own strivings and efforts, now gives itself over to the strong and tender hands of the Lord Jesus and He accepts the task. He immediately begins to work in it *to will and to do of his good pleasure* (Philippians 2:13), delivering it from the tyranny of besetting sin and fulfilling in it His own perfect ideal.

This blessed life should be the normal life of every Christian – at work and rest, in the building up of the inner life, and in the working out of life. This is God's thought not for a few, but for all His children. The youngest and weakest can claim it equally with the strongest and oldest. We should step into it at the moment of conversion without wandering with blistered feet for forty years in the desert, or lying for thirty-eight years with disappointed hopes in the porch of the House of Mercy.

**He asks that we be all for Him – body, soul, and spirit – one reasonable service and gift.**

But since many have long ago passed the moment of conversion without entering the blessed life, it may be best to show clearly what the first step must be to take us within its golden circle. Better take it late than never.

The first step into the blessed life is contained in the one word, *consecration.*

It is enforced by the significant urging of the apostle Paul: *present yourselves unto God as those that are alive from the dead and your members as instruments of righteousness unto God* (Romans 6:13).

It isn't enough to give our time, or energy, or money. Many gladly give anything rather than *themselves*, but none of these will be counted as a sufficient substitute by Him who gave not only His possessions, but also His very self for us. In the same way the Lord Jesus was all for us, He asks that we be all for Him – body, soul, and spirit – one reasonable service and gift. *Therefore,*

*I beseech you brethren, by the mercies of God, that ye present your bodies in living sacrifice, holy, well pleasing unto God, which is your rational worship. And be not conformed to this age, but be ye transformed by the renewing of your soul that ye may experience what is that good and well pleasing and perfect will of God* (Romans 12:1-2).

The fact that consecration is the stepping-stone to blessedness is clearly established in the experience of God's children. For instance, Frances Ridley Havergal has left us this record:

> It was on Advent Sunday, December 1873, that I first saw clearly the blessedness of true consecration. I saw it as a flash of electric light, and what you see you can never unsee. *There must be full surrender before there can be full blessedness. God admits you by the one into the other.* First, I was shown that the blood of Jesus Christ, His Son, cleanseth from all sin; and then it was made plain to me that He who had thus cleansed me, had power to keep me clean; *so I utterly yielded myself to Him and utterly trusted Him to keep me.*

The seraphic Whitfield, the Wesley brothers, the great Welsh preacher Christmas Evans, the French pastor Oberlin, and many more have given the same testimony. And from their mouths this truth may surely be looked upon as established, so that we must pass through Gilgal to the Land of Rest, and the strait gate of consecration alone leads into the blessed life.

## 1. The Ground of Consecration in the Great Scripture Statement Is That We Are Christ's

There is a twofold ground of proprietorship:

a) We are His by purchase. *For ye are bought with a price, therefore glorify God in your body and in your spirit, which are* God's (1 Corinthians 6:20). Step into that slave market where men and women are waiting like possessions to be bought. In the distance you see a wealthy planter coming, who, after appropriate examination, lays down his money for a number of men and women to stock his estate. From that moment on, those people are absolutely his property, as much so as his cattle or his sheep. All they possess, all they may earn, is absolutely his. So, the apostles reasoned, they were Christ's, and often they began their epistles by calling themselves the *slaves of Jesus Christ.* Paul went so far as to say that he bore in his body the brand-marks of Jesus. And aren't all Christians Christ's, whether they own it and live up to it or not, because He purchased them by His most precious blood?

b) We are His also by deed of gift. The Father has given to the Son all who shall come to Him. If you have ever come or will come to Jesus Christ as your Savior, you show that you have been included in that wonderful donation. *All that the Father gives me shall come to me, and he that comes to me I will in no wise cast out*

(John 6:37). Is it likely that the Father gave only a part of us? No, as completely as He gave His Son for us, so has He given us to His Son. And our Lord Jesus thinks a great deal of that solemn transaction; though sadly, we often live as if it never took place and think we are free to live as we please.

2. **The Act of Consecration Is to Recognize Christ's Ownership, and to Accept It, and to Say to Him with the Whole Heart, "Lord, I Am Thine by Right, and I Wish to Be Thine by Choice."**

The mighty men of old of Israel were willing to swim the rivers at their flood stage in order to come to David, their uncrowned but God-appointed king. And when they met him, they cried, "Thine are we, David, and on thy side, thou son of Jesse" (1 Chronicles 12:18). They were his because God had given them to him, but they couldn't rest content until they were his also by their willing choice. Why then shouldn't we say the same to Jesus Christ?

> *Lord Jesus, I am Yours by right. Forgive me that I have lived so long as if I were my own. I now gladly recognize that You have a rightful claim on all I have and am. I want to live as Yours from this time forth, and at this time I solemnly give myself to You. Yours in life and death. Yours absolutely and forever.*

Don't try to make a covenant with God for fear you might break it and be discouraged. Instead, quietly fall into your right attitude as one who belongs to Christ. Take as your motto the noble confession, *whose I am and whom I serve* (Acts 27:23). Breathe the grand, old, simple lines:

> Just as I am,
>     Thy love unknown
> Has broken every barrier down;
>     Now, to be Thine, yea, Thine alone,
> O Lamb of God, I come.

### 3. Consecration Is Not the Act of Our Feelings, But of Our Will

Don't try to feel anything. Don't try to make yourself suitable or good or serious enough for Christ. God is working in you to desire, whether you feel it or not. He is giving you power, at this moment, to want and to do His good pleasure. *For it is God who works in you both to will and to do of his good pleasure* (Philippians 2:13). Believe this, and act upon it at once, and say, "Lord Jesus, I am willing to be Yours"; or, if you can't say as much as that, say, "Lord Jesus, I am willing to be made willing to be Yours forever."

Consecration is only possible when we give up our will *about everything.* As soon as we come to the point of giving ourselves to God, we are almost certain to become aware of the presence of one thing, if not more, that is out of harmony with His will. And while we feel able to surrender ourselves on all other points, here we exercise reservation. Every room and cupboard in the house, with the exception of this, are thrown open to the new occupant. Every limb in the body, except one, is submitted to the practiced hand of the Great Physician. But that small reserve spoils the whole. To give ninety-nine parts and to withhold the hundredth undoes the whole transaction.

Jesus will have all or none. And He is wise. Who would live in a fever-stricken house so long as one room was not exposed to disinfectants, air, and sun? Who would undertake a case so long as the patient refused to submit one part of his body to examination? Who would become responsible for a bankruptcy so long as one ledger was kept back? The reason so many fail to attain the blessed life is that there is one point in which they hold back from God, and concerning which they prefer to have their own way and will rather than His. In this one thing they will not yield their will and accept God's, and this one little thing mars the whole, robs them of peace, and compels them to wander in the desert.

**Jesus will have all or none.**

## 4. If You Cannot Give All, Ask the Lord Jesus to TAKE All, and Especially That Which Seems So Hard to Give

Many have been helped by hearing it put this way: tell them to *give* and they shake their heads despondently. They are like the little child who told her mother that she had been trying to give Jesus her heart, *but it wouldn't go.* But ask them if they are willing for Him to come into their hearts and *take* all, and they will joyfully agree.

Tennyson says, "Our wills are ours to make them Thine." But sometimes it seems impossible to shape them in such a way as to match every corner and angle of the will of God. What a relief it is at such a moment to hand the will over to Christ, telling Him that *we are willing to be made willing* to have His will in all things, and asking Him to melt our stubborn rebelliousness, to fashion our wills on His anvil, and to bring us into perfect harmony with Himself.

### 5. When We Are Willing to Let the Lord Jesus Take All, We Must Believe That He Does Take All

Jesus doesn't wait for us to free ourselves from evil habits, or to make ourselves good, or to feel glad and happy. His one desire is that we put our will on His side in everything. When this is done, He *instantly* enters the surrendered heart and begins His blessed work of renovation and renewal. From the very moment of consecration, even if it is done with much feebleness and little appreciation of its meaning, the spirit can begin to say with emphasis, "I am His! I am His! Glory to God, I am His!" The gift is laid directly on the altar, and the fire falls on it.

Sometimes there is a rush of holy feeling. It was like this in the case of James Brainerd Taylor, who said:

I felt that I needed something which I did not possess. I desired it, not for my benefit only, but for that of the church and the world. I lifted up my heart that the blessing might descend. At this juncture I was most delightfully conscious of giving up ALL to God. I was enabled in my heart to say, "Here, Lord, take me, take my whole soul, and seal me thine – thine now, and thine for ever. If thou wilt, thou canst make me clean." Then there ensued such emotions as I never before experienced – all was calm and tranquil, silent, solemn – and a heaven of love pervaded my whole soul. I had a witness of God's love to me, and of mine to him. Shortly after, I was dissolved in tears of love and gratitude to our blessed Lord. He came as king, and took possession of my heart.

It's delightful when such emotions are granted to us, but we must not look for or depend on them. Our consecration can be accepted and excite the liveliest joy in our Savior's heart, even though we aren't filled with responding ecstasy. We can know with certainty that the great transaction is complete, without any glad outburst of song. We may even have to exercise faith, and go against our feelings, many times each day, and say, "*I* am His." But the absence of feeling proves nothing. We must pillow our heads on the conviction that Jesus took what we gave at the moment of our giving it, and that *he is able to keep that which I have committed unto him against that day* (2 Timothy 1:12).

### 6. We Must Make the Act of Consecration a Definite One in Our Spiritual History

George Whitfield did it in the ordination service: "I can call heaven and earth to witness that when the bishop laid his hands upon me, I gave myself up to be a martyr for Him who hung upon the cross for me. Known unto Him are all the future events and contingences. I have thrown myself blindfolded, and without reserve, into His Almighty hands."

Christmas Evans did it as he was climbing a lonely and mountainous road toward Cader Idris: "I was weary of a cold heart toward Christ and began to pray, and soon felt the fetters loosening. Tears flowed copiously, and I was constrained to cry out for the gracious visits of God. Thus, I resigned myself to Christ, body and soul, gifts and labors, all my life, every day and every hour that remained to me; and all my cares I committed to Christ."

Stephen Grellet did so in the woods: "I had gone into the woods, which are there, mostly, of very lofty and large pines, and my mind being inwardly retired before the Lord, he was pleased so to reveal his love to me, through his blessed Son, my Saviour, that my many fears and doubts were at that time removed, my soul's wounds were healed, my mourning was turned into joy. He strengthened me to offer up myself freely to him and to his service for my whole life."

It matters little when and how we do it – whether by speech or in writing, whether alone or in company – but we must not be content with a general desire. We must come to a definite point, at a given moment of time, when we gladly acknowledge and confess Christ's absolute ownership of all we are and have.

### 7. When the Act of Consecration Is Truly Done, It Need Not Be Repeated

We can look back on this act with thankfulness and may add some new details to it as we learn how much more was involved than we ever dreamed. It is an ongoing process and we may go on to find new areas of our being constantly demanding to be included. But we can't undo it and need never repeat it. And if we fall away from it, let us go at once to our merciful High Priest, confessing our sin and seeking forgiveness and restoration.

### 8. The Advantages Resulting from This Act Cannot Be Enumerated Here

The advantages surpass all count. The first and best is the special filling by the Holy Spirit, and as He fills the heart, He drives out the evil things which held possession there too long before Him, just as mercury, poured into a glass of water, sinks to the bottom, expels the water, and takes its place. We give ourselves directly to Christ, and He seals us by His Spirit. Without delay, we present Him with a yielded nature, and He begins to fill it with the Holy Spirit. Let us not *try* to feel that it is so, but rather let us *believe* that it is so, and reckon on God's faithfulness. Others will soon see a marked difference in us, even though we may have no knowledge of it.

### 9. All We Have to Do Is Maintain This Attitude of Full Surrender by the Grace of the Holy Spirit

Remember that Jesus Christ offered Himself to God *through the eternal Spirit* (Hebrews 9:14), and He waits to do the same for you. Ask Him to maintain you in this attitude, and to maintain this attitude in you. Regularly use the means of meditation, private prayer, and Bible study. Seek forgiveness for any failure as soon as you are conscious of it, and ask to be restored. Practice the godly habit of the constant calling of God to mind. Do not be eager to work for God, but let God work through you. Accept everything that happens to you as being permitted and therefore sent by the will of Him who infinitely loves you. There will roll in upon you wave upon wave, tide upon tide, ocean upon ocean of an experience rightly called the blessed life, because it is full of the happiness of the ever-blessed God Himself.

Dear reader, won't you take this step? When you do, your heart will be filled and satisfied with the true riches. There will be no further difficulty regarding money, clothing, or amusements, or similar things that raise questions and perplex some. As the willing slave of Jesus Christ, you will only seek to do the will of your great and gentle Master. You will long to spend every coin as He directs, to act as His steward, to dress so as to give Him pleasure, to spend your time only in ways He may approve, and to do His will on earth as it is in heaven, and all this will come easily and with delight.

> Seek forgiveness for any failure as soon as you are conscious of it, and ask to be restored.

Perhaps at this time you are far from this, but it is all within your reach. Don't be afraid of Christ. He wants to take nothing from you except the very things you would give up immediately if you could see as clearly as He does the harm they are inflicting. He will ask nothing of you that is inconsistent, and what He asks He will ask with the most perfect appropriateness and tenderness. He will give you grace enough to perform every duty He may demand. His yoke is easy; His burden is light (Matthew 11:30).

Blessed Spirit of God, You alone can use human words to speak to the heart. I pray you will stoop to use these words to point many a longing soul to the first step into the blessed life, for the exceeding glory of the Lord Jesus and for the sake of a dying world.

## Chapter 5

# With Christ in Separation

The Bible rings with the cry for separation. Those words, *Divide! Divide!* so often heard in the House of Commons of England compelling every person to take a side, speak through the pages of the Bible, from those earliest verses which tell how God divided the light from the darkness.

This call came to Abraham, ordering him to leave his home country, his relatives, and his father's house; to Moses, as the bugle note of the Exodus; to the tribe of Levi, mustering them at the gate of the camp; to the children of Israel, as they languished in Babylon, telling them to return to their fatherland; and resounding among the New Testament church, these words re-echoed: *Therefore come out from among them, and be ye separate, saith the Lord, and do not touch the unclean thing; and I will receive you* (2 Corinthians 6:17). *Come out of her, my people, that ye not be partakers of her sins, and that ye receive not of her plagues* (Revelation 18:4).

**What Is That Separation to Which We Are Called?**
Regarding this separation, there are many counterfeits against which we would do well to be on our guard.

*It is not the separation of the monk*
Such separation has always fascinated noble minds. For like-minded men to go off together to some sequestered valley, protected from the storms that sweep across the world, to build for themselves homes and temples, and to work together with holy meditation and prayer, welcoming daybreak with a service of morning prayer and greeting the first starry host with evening prayer and hymns, such was the dream that stirred the imagination of godly hearts in the Middle Ages. And a mindset something like this filled the *Mayflower* with the Pilgrim Fathers, and populated the Black Forest with colonies of Moravian settlers.

No matter how attractive, such separation cannot be the separation of Christ. He solemnly prayed that we might not be taken out of the world. *I do not pray that thou should take them out of the world, but that thou should keep them from the evil* (John 17:15). Indeed, He expressly sent us into the world. And what would happen to the world if we were all to withdraw from its life? It would be a night without a star; a rock-bound coast without a lighthouse beam shining into the murky gloom; a vessel drifting on the rocks without a watch on deck; a carcass spoiling in midsummer without salt! No, this can't be the separation to which we are called.

*It is not the separation of the Pharisee*
The Pharisees supposed a man could be religious without being good. In their view, he could be full of extortion and overindulgence, if he just washed the outside of the cup and the platter. He could be full of dead men's bones, if only he appeared clean like a whitewashed sepulcher. As a result, in their judgment, impurity wasn't a matter of inward evil but something communicated by a touch. To be touched by a man who had not washed since eating would be enough to defile the stately Pharisee.

Our Lord broke down these unrighteous distinctions forever. He taught – not only by what He said but also by His actions – that impurity isn't transferred by physical contact. Unrighteousness is nurtured in the heart and bred in act and speech. Jesus didn't wash after His meals; He ate with publicans and sinners. He let a fallen woman weep at His feet; He touched the bleared eye of blindness, the tied tongue of dumbness, and the diseased flesh of the leper. In all this, we are repeatedly told that He stretched out His hand and touched.

Isn't this what the world needs? It needs a helping hand – the touch of the King. We will never be able to help people by simply looking at them or urging them on. We must *touch* them. Those lily-white, delicate, jeweled hands that may turn this page must be yielded to Christ, so He can use them and work His miracles of mercy through them in our weary age. Such contact will not defile. In fact, when we dare to make the contact in the name of Christ and for the welfare of a dying world, it is a disinfectant so far from defiling that it tends to promote our love for purity.

*It is not the separation of the Stoic*
The Puritans were not entirely free from this mistake. For them, the world was a great, howling wilderness. In their eyes, laughter and merriment were signs of an unregenerate soul. Their plan for life was too narrow and severe to welcome those lighter and softer passages which relieve its strain and draw out the tenderer sentiments of human hearts.

Christ's life was a perpetual protest against this. He mingled with wedding guests, smiled at the children as they played in the marketplaces and called to their companions. He directed the attention of the crowds to the beauties of the flowers and the habits of the birds. He noticed the sunrise hues and evening tints in the sky and lived as a man among them. However severe He might have seemed to the people of His time who observed appearances only without possessing the life and spirit of religion, He always had a warm heart toward what was natural and human. Let's not forget the command, *Thou shalt rejoice in every good thing which the LORD thy God has given unto thee* (Deuteronomy 26:11), and let us cultivate the habit of extracting joy and blessing from all the innocent and beautiful things around us.

> Let us cultivate the habit of extracting joy and blessing from all the innocent and beautiful things around us.

## The Necessity of Answering This
## Question Is Really Urgent

Hundreds of young Christians are asking what they should do or avoid. It is a *pressing* question, and in so many cases, they begin to drift because of a lack of a clear principle. As a result, the bloom passes off the basket of summer fruit, and once it is gone, it can never be replaced. It is a *pertinent* question, especially at those times of year when the dark evenings allow such abundant opportunities for the dance, the ball, the theater, and the opera.

It is also a *perplexing* question, because good people are found on such opposite sides and give answers as wide apart as the poles to the various questions with which they are provided. Some forbid the theater but allow the opera. Some have no objection to the children's pantomime, but are horrified at the proposal of seeing an ordinary play. Some would go to see Shakespearean plays but won't go to others. Some distinguish between a dance and a ball.

What is the result? Christian ministers frequent theaters. Professing Christians give dancing parties not far removed from balls. Funds for religious purposes are raised by private dramatic performances. Our young people are perpetually loosening the restraints that hold them by pushing the fences which divide them from the world outward, taking in new spans of territory, and fussing against restraint.

Are there no principles on which Christians act, without external influence or control, so that each individual soul can decide for itself these difficult, doubtful, and perilous problems which are so incessantly cropping up in all our lives in one form or another? In truth, there are, and the following principles are surely among them, and, like the spear of the seraph Ithuriel, these will indicate by a touch the evil that may lurk under innocent appearances:

## 1. Beware of Anything Inconsistent in Your Relationship with the Lord Jesus

What is that relationship? Of course, here we are talking about those who are His alone, or who are desirous of being identified with Him, both now and in the future.

*We are His servants*, bought by His blood, and sworn to loyal allegiance. Isn't it consistent then to consider the amusements and gaieties of the world to be of the same spirit today as when it cast Him out of its camp and crucified Him? It has an ugly look about it when loyal soldiers fraternize in the celebrations of rebels.

*We are His members*, bone of His bone, flesh of His flesh, whom He nourishes and cherishes. Our Head is already passed through the grave on to resurrection ground, where He is gathering His own people around Him. Isn't it inconsistent then for the Head to be on one side of the grave and the members of the body on the other? Isn't it totally improper to pretend to be one with Him in His risen glory, while in practice we are as close as we dare live in our contact with the world which He has left?

*We are His bride.* He, the heavenly Bridegroom, is one with us in a union which has no comparison except that of wedlock where heart unites with heart. Is it consistent with faithfulness to Him for us to hang around with the world, whose hands are saturated with His blood? What did the people of Scotland think of the intimate associations of marriage between Mary, Queen of Scots and Bothwell, the murderer of her first husband, Lord Darnley?

Surely, the outstretched arms of the cross bar the bridge between us and the world. We can cry with the apostle Paul, *But in no wise should I glory, except in the cross of our Lord Jesus Christ, by whom the world is crucified unto me, and I unto the world* (Galatians 6:14).

Whenever there is any doubt as to whether it is right to go to this place or that, bring the question under the light that streams from the cross and from the throne. Clear your heart and mind of all selfish purposes and thoughts of what other people might do or say. Let your eyes be discerning to single out the will of the Lord. Ask what He would have you do. Before long, the difficulties will roll up as quickly and quietly as the mists that fill the mountain valleys before the touch of the summer sun. Your whole body will be full of light. *The lamp of the body is the eye: if therefore thine eye is sincere, thy whole body shall be full of light* (Matthew 6:22). You will even lose the taste for things you once loved. And in the newfound ecstasy of the living water welling up in your heart, you will be prepared to leave behind the water pot that you had relied on as the source of your life.

> Clear your heart and mind of all selfish purposes and thoughts of what other people might do or say.

## 2. Beware of Anything Which the World Itself Deems Inconsistent

Though the world isn't religious in our sense, it still has a very keen appreciation of true Christianity and a very high ideal of what Christians should be. And when we are met with unexpected questioning such as, "What! Are you here? We didn't expect to see you!" then we should aptly halt our steps, because the very fuss made over us when we step over the line might suitably make us pause and ask whether or not we've done something to forfeit the smile and the "*Well done*" of Jesus (Matthew 25:21).

## 3. Beware of Anything Which Could Injure Some Weaker Conscience

This is one of the most important considerations in Christian living.

*All things are lawful unto me, but all things are not expedient* (1 Corinthians 6:12). And why aren't they expedient? It is inexpedient or unwise to do things that might seem harmless enough in themselves and which you might feel free to do, if in doing them you lead others to also do them, not because they feel comfortable doing them, but simply because they are emboldened by your example, since they regard you as further advanced in the Christian life than themselves, and so a trustworthy guide.

Evaluate every action – not only the action itself but also how it is likely to influence others – for fear that by your example you may break down decent moral barriers and place other people in positions of temptation, which, however harmless to yourself, are perilous in the extreme to them. We have no right to lead our young children up perilous roads, where *we* may clamber with clear head and nimble foot, but where *their* inexperienced steps may slide into the abyss.

## 4. Beware of Settings and Friendships Which Dull Your Spiritual Life

Who doesn't long for a life on fire for the Lord? But how can we possibly expect such a thing if we persistently expose ourselves to influences that choke it and repress it and damp it down? Before we retire to rest, some settings seem incompatible with sincere prayer and Bible study. Such places lower the inner spiritual temperature and leave a bad flavor in the mouth. They poison the young life in the same way noxious gas fumes poison the life of flowers and plants. It is best for us to refrain our feet from all such places.

## 5. Beware of Any Company with People Who Make You Feel Compelled to Put a Bushel over Your Testimony

We must shine like lights in the world. *Ye are the light of the world* (Matthew 5:14).

The most necessary condition in a lighthouse lamp is its permanence. If it shines one time but is hidden at another time, if it flashes far over the dark, angry waves and then stands dull and obscure on the prominent jutting cliff, of what use is it? It is worse than useless. And if we are to be of any real use in this world, our testimony for Jesus must be maintained in season and out of season, in storm and sunshine, always and everywhere. But if you have to remind yourself that you must not touch on any of those subjects dearest to your soul before going into any situation or group of people, you may well be apprehensive for fear you are trespassing on forbidden ground. Go no place where you can't take Jesus with you, and ask His blessing before going. *Do everything for the glory of God* (1 Corinthians 10:31).

All of this will involve hard fighting, persecution, and misunderstanding. However, it is in this way that we prove our lineage with the noble martyr spirits of the past. See that young girl in the days of Diocletian, beautiful and richly dressed, standing before the altar with the judge on one side, her lover on the other, with her companions grouped around. If she will only throw a few grains of incense on the fire, she will be spared from cruel death and given back to love and friends and life. But not a single grain is cast upon the expectant flames, and she is ruthlessly led off to die for Him whom she loves more than all. Wasn't she consistent? Wouldn't you have done the same? Then do the same now and dare to be consistent to your lover, Christ.

At times we may be placed in a position where we have no alternative other than to go into a situation we wouldn't choose for ourselves. For instance, when the worldly mother of a Christian girl insists on her accompanying her into society, where there is nothing positively sinful but much that is light and thoughtless, it would likely be her responsibility to go. In such a situation, you can ask to be excused, but if permission isn't granted, you must go, unless conscience positively forbids, and Christ will go with you keeping your heart.

## There Are Many Advantages

This is the only *safe* choice. The world is so attractive and appeals to our weaknesses in such a way that if we launch upon its waters once, they will sweep us toward the rush of the whirlpool in a manner not felt or perceived, and we will go down into the deep, dark abyss.

It is the only *strong* course. He who wants to lift me must stand above me. Who did the most for Sodom? Was it Lot who went down into it and sat in the gate, or Abraham who got up early to go to the place where he stood before the Lord? The old pagan games were swept off the world, not because the early Christians went to them but

> He who wants to lift me must stand above me.

because they stayed away. The brutal sports of the last century fell out of favor and went away, not because the Methodists patronized them but because they abstained from them. The same holds true for the moral pests of modern society. They will never go away until good people withdraw both their patronage and support.

This is the only *blessed* course because God's promise of being a Father and of receiving us is entirely dependent on our complying with His conditions. It is when father and mother forsake us that the Lord gathers us. When the synagogue casts us out, Jesus finds us; when heart and flesh fail, He is the strength of our heart and our portion forever (Psalm 73:26).

Dare to go outside the camp, at the risk of being

thought of as odd and unfriendly. Let the world treat you like it treated your Lord. Why would the servant be stroked and flattered when the Master was crucified as a felon? Lie in His grave and, in this way, you will know the joys of His resurrection life, the sweetness of His love, and the closeness of His friendship, which will compensate for a thousand deaths. To know the King, you must share His exile.

Gather ye, gather ye, out to the lone cave of Adullam, and around the standard of the exiled Prince; and when He comes again in triumph to be crowned with the diadem of universal empire, ye shall appear in His train and by His side, confessed and acknowledged as those of whom He has no reason to be ashamed.

## Chapter 6

# How to Read Your Bible

Christian living, in my opinion, completely hinges on the way Christian people read the Bible for themselves. All sermons and lectures, all Bible readings and classes, and all religious magazines and books can never take the place of our own quiet study of God's precious Word. We can measure our growth in grace by the growth of our love for private Bible study, and we can be sure something is seriously wrong when we lose our appetite for the Bread of Life. Perhaps we have been eating too many sweets, or exercising too little, or breathing too briefly in the bracing air which sweeps over the uplands of spiritual fellowship with God.

Those of us who have learned the blessed art of discovering the treasures of the Bible for ourselves are happy to find those gems hidden just a little below the surface, so as to test our real sincerity in finding them. No specimens are as interesting as those which the naturalist has obtained by his own efforts – each of which has a history.

No flowers are so fragrant as those which we discover for ourselves nestled in some woodland glade secluded from the eye and step of men. No pearls are as priceless as those which we have sought for ourselves in the calm, clear depths of the ocean of truth. Only those who know it can realize the joy that fills the spirit when one makes a great "find" in some previously unseen connection, some fresh reference, or some railway line from verse to verse.

A few simple rules can help many more people acquire this holy skill, and here I endeavor to write them down. May the Holy Spirit Himself own and use them.

### 1. Make Time for Bible Study

The divine Teacher must have preset and uninterrupted hours for meeting His scholars. His Word must have our freshest and brightest thoughts. We must give Him our best and the firstfruits of our days. That's why there's no time for Bible study like the early morning. After we have opened our letters, glanced through the paper, and joined in the prattle of the breakfast table, we can't give such undivided attention to the holy thoughts that glisten like diamonds on the pages of Scripture. When the Israelites of old gathered the manna, it had to be done before the dew evaporated and the sun was up, otherwise it melted. *And they gathered it early in the morning, each one according to his eating; and when the sun waxed hot, it melted* (Exodus 16:21).

For that reason, we should aim at ensuring at least half an hour before breakfast for the leisurely and loving study of the Bible. To some this might seem like a long time compared with what they give now. But soon it will seem all too short. The more you read the Bible, the more you will want to read it. It is an appetite which grows as it is fed.

And you will be repaid well. The Bible seldom speaks to those who always read it in a hurry, and certainly never speaks of its deepest, sweetest words. Nature can only tell her secrets to people who will sit still in her sacred temple until their eyes lose the glare of earthly glory, and their ears are attuned to her voice. And will divine revelation do what nature cannot? Never. The man who will win the heavenly joys of hearing her must watch daily at her gates and wait at the posts of her doors. There is no chance for a young man to grow who only gets an occasional mouthful of food and always swallows it in a hurry.

Of course, this time before breakfast isn't possible for everyone. The invalid, the nurse with broken rest, the public servant whose shift often turns night into day – these are exceptions and the Lord Jesus can make it up to them. If needs be, He shall sit with them at midday beside the well. In the case of such people who can only snatch a few words of Scripture as they hurry to their work, the miracle of the manna will be repeated. *He that gathered much had nothing over*; that is, all we get in our morning reading isn't "too much" for the needs of the day. *And he that gathered little had no lack* (Exodus 16:18); that is, when circumstances compel and we are unable to do more than snatch up a hasty handful of manna, it will last us all through the day. *The pitcher of meal shall not be consumed, neither shall the cruse of oil fail* (1 Kings 17:14).

It would be impossible to name everyone who has traced their usefulness and power to this priceless habit. Sir Henry Havelock always spent the first two hours of each day alone with God, and if the camp turned out at 6:00 a.m., he would rise at 4:00 a.m. Earl Cairns rose daily at six o'clock to guarantee an hour and a half for the study of the Bible and for prayer before conducting family worship at a quarter to eight, even when the late hours of the House of Commons left him with no more than two hours' sleep. It is the practice of a beloved missionary friend of mine to spend at least three hours each morning with his Bible. He has said that he often puts aside pressing engagements so that he not only can have time but also be fresh for it.

It's no doubt difficult to awaken early enough to get time for our Bible before breakfast, but these difficulties present no barrier to those who must leave early for work or activities of pleasure. If we *mean* to get up, we *can* get up. Of course, we must prepare for early rising by retiring early enough to get our needed rest, even though it might cost some cozy hours by the fireside on the winter's night. But with suitable forethought and fixed purpose, the thing can surely be done. *All things are possible to him that believes* (Mark 9:23).

I will never forget seeing Charles Studd early one

November morning, clothed in flannels to protect himself from the cold, and rejoicing that the Lord had awakened him at 4:00 a.m. to study His commands. He told me it was his custom to trust the Lord to call him and enable him to rise. Couldn't we all do this? The weakest *can do all things through Christ who strengthens* (Philippians 4:13). And though you have failed again and again when you trusted your own resolutions, you can't fail when you simply trust Him. *He wakes up early, early shall he awaken my ear, that I might hear* (Isaiah 50:4). *And he took him by the right hand and lifted him up, and immediately his feet and ankle bones received strength* (Acts 3:7).

## 2. Look Up for the Teaching of the Holy Spirit

No one can explain the meaning of his words as well as the person who wrote them. Tennyson could best explain some of his deeper references in his *In Memoriam*. If you want to read the Bible as you should, then make much of the Holy Spirit who inspired it through holy men. As you open the book, lift up your heart and say, *Open my eyes, and I shall behold the wonders of thy law* (Psalm 119:18), and say, *Speak; for thy slave hears* (1 Samuel 3:10).

The light commentaries cast on the inner meaning of Scripture are marvelous but meager compared to what the simple-hearted believer, depending on the aid of the Holy Spirit, will find in the Bible, because they will discover what the wisest have mistaken or missed. The apostle John said as much: *Ye do not need that anyone teach you; but as the same anointing teaches you of all things and is truth* (1 John 2:27). What fire is to invisible ink, bringing the colorless fluid out black and clear, the teaching of the Holy Spirit is to passages in the Bible which had seemed meaningless and bare.

We can never know too much about literature which throws sidelights on the Bible, and which unfolds the customs of the people, difficult allusions, historical coincidences, or geographical details. Geikie's *Hours with the Bible*, Kitto's *Daily Bible Illustrations*, and Dr. William Smith *Smith's Bible Dictionary* are invaluable books like these. But we should study them at another time other than the sacred morning hour we give to the Holy Spirit alone.

### 3. Read the Bible Methodically

On the whole, there's probably no better way than to read through the Bible once every year. There is a very good plan for doing this in the life of the godly M'Cheyne, who drew it up for his people. Or it may be done in a *Bagster's Bible Handbook* by daily taking three columns of the Old Testament, two of the New Testament, and one of the Psalms. This system will more than do it.

The next best plan is the one adopted by Mr. Richardson's Bible Reading Union, which consists of tens of thousands of Christians in every part of the world who read one chapter a day in regular rotation to get through the Bible in about three years.

It is wise to have a good quality copy of the Scriptures, strongly bound for wear and tear, with good clear print, and with as much space as possible for notes – a book you can make a friend and inseparable companion. But above all, in the beginning, it's wise to select one with abundant marginal references making it easy to turn to parallel passages. For myself, this plan has infused my Bible reading with new interest. I love to have one of the paragraph Bibles from the Religious Tract Society in front of me. It abounds with well-chosen references. I also like to have a small pocket Bible in my hand, so I can easily turn to any reference I desire.

> **It is sometimes best to read a book of the Bible in a sitting, devoting two or three hours to the sacred task.**

Very often I get more blessing from the passages I refer to, and those to which these lead, than from the one I may be reading.

After a while, we begin to make references for ourselves. At this point, we can use a copy of the Revised Bible, so we can not only enjoy the immense advantage of reading God's Word in the most approved English rendering, but so that we can also have the opportunity to fill the empty margins with notes about parallel passages.

But whatever system is adopted, *be sure to read the Bible through on some system, as you would any other book*. No one would think of reading a letter, a poem, or history like many read God's Word. It's no wonder they are so ignorant about its majestic prose, its exquisite lyric poetry, its massive arguments, its sublime imagery, its spiritual beauty – qualities which combine to make it the King of Books, even though the halo of inspiration didn't shine like a crown about its brow.

It is sometimes best to read a book of the Bible in a sitting, devoting two or three hours to the sacred task. At other times, it is more profitable to take an era, or an episode, or a life, and compare all that is written about it in various parts of Scripture. At other times, again, it is best to follow the plan which Mr. Moody has so often insisted, of taking one word or thought, such as *faith*, or *love*, or *able*, and tracing it with the help of a concordance, from end to end of the inspired Book. But in any case, let the *whole* Bible be your study, because *all scripture is given by inspiration of God and is profitable for doctrine, for reproof, for correction, for instruction in righteousness* (2 Timothy 3:16). Even the rocky places shall gush with springs of water. The most barren chapters shall blossom like the rose. *Out of the eater came forth food, and out of the strong came forth sweetness* (Judges 14:14).

> Let the Bible be its own dictionary, its own interpreter, its own best commentary.

Let us never forget that the Bible is one Book; it is the work of one infinite Spirit, speaking through prophet and priest, shepherd and king, the old-world patriarch and the apostle who lived to see Jerusalem leveled to the ground. You can subject its words to the most thorough test, but you will find they always have the same meaning and move in the same direction. Let the Bible be its own dictionary, its own interpreter, its own best commentary. It is like a vast, buried city in which every turn of the spade reveals some new wonder, while passages branch off in every direction calling for exploration.

## 4. Read Your Bible with Your Pen in Hand

Writing about F. R. Havergal, her sister says, "She read her Bible at her study table by seven o'clock in the summer, and eight o'clock in winter. Sometimes, on bitterly cold mornings, I begged that she would read with her feet comfortably to the fire, and received the reply: 'But then, Marie, I can't rule my lines neatly; just see what a find I've got! If only one searches, there are such extraordinary things in the Bible!' She resolutely refrained from late hours and frittering talks at night, in place of Bible searching and holy communings. Early rising and early studying were her rule through life."

In my judgment, no one has learned the secret of enjoying the Bible until they have started to mark it, neatly. Underlining and dating special verses, which have cast light on their path on distinctive days. Drawing connections, across the pages, between verses which repeat the same message, or ring with the same note. Jotting down new references, or the catchwords of helpful thoughts. All these methods find plenty to occupy the pen and fix our treasures for us permanently. Our Bible then becomes the precious memento of bygone hours, and records the history of our inner life.

## 5. Seek Eagerly Your Personal Profit

Don't read the Bible for others, for class or congregation, but for yourself. Bring all its rays to a focus on your own heart. While you're reading, ask often that some verse or verses may jump out from the printed page as God's message to you. Never close the Book until you feel you are carrying away your portion of meat from that hand which satisfies the desire of every living thing. Sometimes it is best to stop reading and to seriously ask, "What does the Holy Spirit mean for *me* to learn from this? What influence should this have on *my* life? How can I work this into the fabric of *my* character?"

Don't let the Bible simply be like a history book, a treatise, or a poem to you, but look at it as your Father's letter to you –a letter which offers some things you won't understand until you come into the circumstances that require them, but a letter which is also full of present help. There's a great difference between the way a child away from home scans through newspapers versus the way he devours the letter from home through which the beloved parent speaks. Both are interesting, but the one is general, and the other is totally written to him. Read the Bible, not like a newspaper, but as a letter from home.

### 6.  Above All, Turn from the Printed Page to Prayer

If a cluster of heavenly fruit hangs within reach, gather it. If a promise lies on the page of scripture like a blank check, cash it. If a prayer is recorded, adopt it as your own and launch it like a feathered arrow from the bow of your desire. If an example of holiness shines before you, ask God to do as much for you. If a truth is revealed in all its intrinsic splendor, pray that its brilliance may always light the hemisphere of your life like a star. Interweave the climbing creepers of holy desire about the latticework of Scripture, and you will come to say with the psalmist, *O how I love thy law! It is my meditation all the day.* (Psalm 119:97).

It is sometimes best to read over Psalm 119 while on our knees; it's so full of devout love for the Bible. And if any want to scold us for spending so much time on the Old Testament, or the New, let us remind them of the words of Christ: *It is written, Man shall not live by bread alone, but by every word that proceeds out of the mouth of God* (Matthew 4:4). The Old Testament must be worth our study since it was our Savior's Bible, deeply pondered and often quoted. And the New Testament demands it, since it is so full of what He said and did, not only in His earthly life, but also through His holy apostles and prophets.

### Advantages of a Deep Knowledge of the Bible

The advantages of having a deep knowledge of the Bible are more than can be numbered here. It is the storehouse of the promises. It is the sword of the Spirit, before which temptation flees. It is the all-sufficient equipment intended for Christian usefulness. It is the believer's guidebook and directory in all possible circumstances. Words fail to tell how glad, how strong, how useful the daily life will be for those who can say with the prophet: *Thy words were found, and I ate them; and thy word was unto me the joy and rejoicing of my heart* (Jeremiah 15:16).

### Practice What You Learn

One thing should be said after everything else, because it is most important and should linger in the memory and heart even if all the other advice of this chapter should pass away like a summer brook. It is this: it is useless to dream of making headway in the knowledge of Scripture unless we are prepared to practice each new and clearly defined responsibility which looms out before our view. We are taught, not just for our pleasure, but also that we may do what it says. *But be ye doers of the word, and not hearers only, deceiving your own selves* (James 1:22). Through the dear grace of Jesus Christ our Lord, if we turn each holy precept or command into instant obedience, God will keep nothing back from us. He will open His deepest and sweetest thoughts to us, but as long as we refuse to obey even the smallest command, we will find that the light will fade from the pages of Scripture, and the enthusiasm will die down quickly in our own hearts.

> *This book of the law shall not depart out of thy mouth, but thou shalt meditate therein day and night that thou may keep and do according to all that is written therein; for then thou shalt make thy way to prosper.*
> (Joshua 1:8)

## Chapter 7

# Monotony and Purpose

A young friend, richly gifted, but tied by unavoidable necessity to an office stool, has complained to me that his life afforded no outlet for the suitable exercise of his abilities.

His complaint is a very common one. Many grumble about the monotony of life's average moments, which the great majority of us have to deal with. The upland paths which provide an ecstatic walk in the stimulating air and the expanding glory of the world are for the few. For most of us, life walks the trivial round and knows the common task. Each morning the bell calls to the same routine of commonplace work. Each hour brings the same program of trivialities. It feels as if there's no chance for doing anything heroic, anything which will be worth having lived for, or which will shed a light back on all past days, and forward on all coming days.

But there are two or three considerations, which,

if worked into the heart, will tend to remove much of this terrible depression.

### 1. All Life Is Part of a Divine Plan

In the same way a mother desires the best possible for her babes as she bends over the cradle which each occupies in turn, so God desires to do His best for all of us. He hates nothing He has made but has a fair ideal for each, which He desires to accomplish in us with perfect love. But there is no way of transferring it to our actual experience, except by the touch of His Spirit internally and by what we learn from our circumstances externally.

He has chosen the circumstances of our life because they are the shortest path, if only we use them as we should to reach the goal on which He has set His heart. He might have chosen some other country – China, India, Italy, or Mexico. He might have chosen some other age – that of the flood, the exodus, or of the early martyrs. He might have chosen some other lot – a royal court, a senate, a pulpit, or an author's desk. But since He chose this land, this age, and your lot (whatever it may be), we must believe that these presented the likeliest and swiftest way for realizing His purpose.

If, my brother, you could have reached your truest manhood as an emperor or a reformer, or as a millionaire or a martyr, then you would have been born into one of those positions. But since you are only a servant, a bank clerk, or an ordinary businessman, you will find the materials and possibilities of a great life right beside you.

If, my sister, you could have reached the grandest development of your nature by being a mother, or a rich man's wife, or a queen, then you would have found yourself placed there. But since your lot is that of a hatmaker's assistant, a factory hand, or a toiling mother, you must believe that somewhere within your reach, if only you search for them, you will discover the readiest conditions of a noble and useful life.

Who can wonder at the complaints of the purposelessness, the futility, the weariness of life? People either have no plan, or they have a wrong plan. "What's the fashion?" "What do others do?" "What's the correct thing?" How much better and wiser to believe that God has a perfect plan for each of us, and that He is unfolding it a bit at a time by the events He puts into our life each day!

Before Moses built the tabernacle, he saw the whole pattern of it in a prophetic vision. In some secluded spot on Sinai's heights, it stood before him, woven out of sunbeams, and he descended to the foot of the mountain to repeat it in actual curtains, gold, and wood. God usually doesn't show us the whole plan of our life in a single burst, but unfolds it to us bit by bit. Each day He gives us the opportunity of weaving a curtain, carving a peg, or fashioning the metal. We don't recognize what we do, but at the end of our life, the disjointed pieces will suddenly come together, and we shall see the symmetry and beauty of the divine thought. At that point, we will

> God usually doesn't show us the whole plan of our life in a single burst, but unfolds it to us bit by bit.

be satisfied. In the meantime, let us believe that God's love and wisdom are doing the very best for us. In the morning, ask God to show you His plan for the day in the unfolding of its events, and to give you grace to do or bear all He may have prepared. In the midst of the day's engagements, often look up and say, "Father, is this in the plan?" At night, be still, and match your actual actions with God's ideal, confessing your sins and shortcomings, and asking that His will may be more perfectly done in you, even as in heaven.

## 2. Every Life Presents Opportunities for Building Up Noble Character

We are sent into this world to build up characters which will be blessed and useful in that great future for which we are being trained. There is a niche which only we can fill, a crown which only we can wear, music which only we can rouse, service which only we can supply. God knows what these are, and He is giving us opportunities to prepare for them. Life is our schoolhouse. Its rooms may be bare, but they are littered with opportunities of becoming ready to go for our great inheritance.

Knitting needles are cheap and common enough, but the most beautiful designs in the richest wools can be fashioned on them. In the same way, the incidents of daily life may be commonplace in the extreme, but as the material foundation, we may build on them the unseen but everlasting fabric of a noble and beautiful character. It doesn't matter so much what we do, but the way in which we do it matters greatly. What we do may or may not live on, but the way in which we perform our common tasks becomes an indestructible part of our character, for better or worse, and forever.

Suppose we meet the daily demands of life with a sloppy and careless spirit, caring only to escape blame, to earn our wage, or to maintain a decent average. Or suppose our one goal in life is to obtain money for our own enjoyment. Isn't it clear that the lack of excellence or dignity of the motive will react on the whole character behind it? In such a case where the soul is always bathed in such an atmosphere and confronted with such ideals, won't it be certain and inevitable that it will become sloppy, careless, greedy, and selfish? And when some great occasion arises, it will call in vain for the high qualities of a noble nature.

On the other hand, suppose we take on the little responsibilities of life faithfully, punctually, thoughtfully, and reverently – not for the praise of man, but for the "*Well done*" of Christ. Not for the payment we might receive, but because God has given us a little piece of work to do in His great world. Not because we must, but because we choose to do it – not as the slaves of circumstances, but as Christ's freed ones. In this way, far beneath the flow of everyday life, the foundations of a character are laid, more beautiful and enduring than coral, and which presently rears itself before the eyes of men and angels and becomes an emerald isle, green with perennial beauty, and vocal with the songs of Paradise.

For that reason, we should be very careful how we fulfill the commonplace tasks of daily life. We are building the character in which we will spend eternity. We are either building into ourselves wood, hay, and stubble, which will have to be burned out at great cost, or the gold, silver, and precious stones which will be things of beauty and joy forever. *Now if anyone builds upon this foundation gold, silver, precious stones, wood, hay, stubble, the work of each one shall be made manifest, for the day shall declare it because it shall be revealed by fire; the work of each one, whatever sort it is, the fire shall put it to test* (1 Corinthians 3:12-13).

## 3. The Great Doing of Little Things Will Make a Great Life

Let's say you are a person of ordinary ability, and languishing like a wood-bird in its cage. It's likely you will never move into a wider sphere than the obscure one you have been in. Give up your useless regret, your discontented complaint, and begin to meet the call of the insignificant and ordinary with faith in God that He is doing His best for you. Meet the call with tenderness to each person you encounter with heroic courage and unswerving fidelity, with patience, thoroughness, and submission.

Go on acting in this way week in and week out, year by year, with no thought about what other people think, determined always to be your best, eager only to pay out without holding back the gold of a noble, unselfish heart. At the end of life, though you don't realize that your face glows, others will see you shining like the sun in your heavenly Father's kingdom. At that time, you will discover that you have unwittingly lived a great life, and you will be greeted on the threshold of heaven with the "*Well done*" of your Lord.

Some who long for a great life are unconsciously living it in the eyes of God's angels. Those who forego marriage so they can bring up and educate the younger children in their family; those who deny themselves almost the necessities of life to add some coals of comfort to the meager fire at which the chill hands of age warm themselves; those who are not only pure themselves amid temptation, but who are also centers of purity, shielding others; those who stand at their post of duty though the fires as they creep near scorch the skin and consume the heart; those who meet the incessant demand of monotonous tasks with gentleness, unselfishness, and the wealth of a strong, true heart – these, even though they don't know it, are graduating toward the front ranks of heaven's nobility.

> "Oh! where is the sea?" the fishes cried,
>     As they swam the crystal clearness through;
> "We've heard from of old of the ocean's tide,
>     And we long to look on the water's blue.
> The wise ones speak of the infinite sea.
>     Oh, who can tell us if such there be?"
>
> The lark flew up in the morning bright,
>     And sang and balanced on sunny wings;
> And this was its song: "I see the light,
>     I look o'er the world of beautiful things;
> But flying and singing everywhere,
>     In vain I have searched to find the air."[6]

---

6    Minot J. Savage, "Where is God?" in *Poems* (Boston, MA: G. H. Ellis, 1882).

### 4. It Is a Greater Thing to do Little Things Well, than Those Which Seem More Important

People who daily handle matters largely before the eyes of their companions are expected to act from excellent motives and to conduct themselves in a manner worthy of their great and important positions. *I therefore, the prisoner of the Lord, beseech you that ye walk worthy of the vocation with which ye are called* (Ephesians 4:1). The statesman is expected to have strong moral principles, the Christian lady to be virtuous, and the minister to be earnest. There is no special credit to any of these people for being what they profess and are expected to be. The current is with them. Their difficulty is to face it.

But surely, in God's sight, it is a much greater thing when the soul conquers adverse circumstances and rises above the drift of its associations instead of going with the flow. To maintain high moral principles when your companions are uncaring and degrading; to be chaste, when ease and wealth beckon for you to enter the gate of sin; to be devout or zealous, when no one expects it; to do small things from excellent motives – this is the grandest accomplishment of the soul.

It is a greater thing to do an unimportant thing from an excellent motive, for God, for truth, and for others, than to do an important one. It is greater to suffer a thousand stings patiently each day, than die once as a martyr at the stake. And for that reason an obscure life really offers more opportunities for the nurture of the noblest type of character, just because it is less liable to be visited by those selfish considerations of notoriety, applause, or money, which intrude into more prominent positions and scatter their deadly corruption.

## 5. Little Things Greatly Done Prepare for the Right Doing of Great Things

We sometimes lay down the storybook or the history book with a groan. We have been reading about some sudden opportunity which came to a Grace Darling[7] reared in the obscurity of a fisherman's home, or to a Florence Nightingale, or a John Brown, living apart from the great world in the heart of the Adirondacks. "Oh," we say, "if only such a chance would dip down into my life, and lift me out of it! I'm weary, weary of this dull existence."

Sadly, this is a common mistake. People think the opportunity makes the hero, but it only reveals him.

In mining, tracing the appearance of a lode or mineral to its head must begin long before, and be done carefully, or else the falling of a single spark would never blast the mighty rocks or shiver the threatening fortress walls. The fabric of strong and noble character must be built up by patient endurance

> **People think the opportunity makes the hero, but it only reveals him.**

in well-doing, or else the sudden appeal of the critical hour will knock unsuccessfully at the door of life, and the soul will crouch helpless inside without an answer.

If great opportunities were to come to most of us, we would make nothing of them. They would pass us by unnoticed or unimproved. They would bypass us and

---

7    A legendary Victorian heroine (1815-1842).

go to those with more nerve, grit, or spiritual power than us. You can not, at will, speak a foreign language, or dash off a brilliant air upon the piano, or talk easily on the motive of one of Browning's poems. All of these goals demand long and arduous study. That must be given the first slot in the management of your time; that way if a call for any of them comes suddenly as you watch for opportunities, you will be ready.

You can't be brave in a crisis if you are habitually a coward. You can't be generous with a fortune if you are a miser with a limited income. You can't be unselfish in some such accident which imperils life if you are always pressing for the one vacant seat in the train or omnibus, and elbowing your way to the front in every possible situation. David had to practice with sling and stone through long hours in the wilderness, or he would never have brought down Goliath. Joseph had to be pure in thought and strong in private self-discipline, or he would never have resisted the solicitations of the temptress. The Sunday school teacher must be regular, painstaking, and faithful in conducting his class of little ragged boys, or he will never be promoted to serve his Master as a pastor or as a missionary.

> You can't be brave in a crisis if you are habitually a coward.

## 6. Our Behavior in Little Things Is the Truest Test of What We Are

If I were eager to acquire a good employee for a responsible position, I wouldn't attach much importance to the way in which the candidate acted on a set occasion during which he knew he was being observed, because, of course, he would be on his best behavior. But give me a private window so I can watch him in his least-considered actions – how he behaves at home, how he treats his mother and sisters, how he fulfills the ordinary duties of life. What he is then, he is really.

But if this is man's way, might it not be God's way? In eternity, great tasks are to be fulfilled: angels to be judged, cities to be ruled, perhaps worlds to be evangelized. Suitable representatives will be required for these opportunities: those who can rule because they have served, those who can command because they have obeyed, those who can save others because they never saved themselves. Perhaps, even now, our heavenly Father is engaged in seeking those among us who can fill these posts. And He is seeking them not among people like those filling high positions in the eyes of men, but rather He is looking within the ranks of people walking the insignificant routine and fulfilling the ordinary task.

From the nearest fixed star, the inequalities of our earth, whether of Alp or molehill, are similarly insignificant. We need to look at our positions from the standpoint of eternity, and when we do, we'll probably be surprised at the small differences between the lots in life of people. The one thing for all of us is to abide in our calling with God, to count ourselves as His fellow workers, to do what we can in His grace and for His glory, never excusing ourselves, never condoning failure or wrongdoing, never content unless, by the help of the blessed Spirit, we have worked out His promptings and suggestions to the best of our ability, whether in the gold of the extraordinary or the bronze of the cheaper and more ordinary achievement.

Of course, there is no saving merit in what we do. Salvation comes only through simple trust in our Savior, Jesus. But when we are saved, it gives new zest to life to do everything for Him, as Lord and Master, and to know that He is well pleased in our rightly doing the most trivial duties at home or in daily business.

> *For what glory is it if, when ye are buffeted*
> *for your faults, ye shall take it patiently? but*
> *if, when ye do well and suffer for it, ye take*
> *it patiently, this is due to grace from God.*
> (1 Peter 2:20)

May each reader learn this happy skill and go through life offering everything to God, like the priests dressed in white stoles in the temple of old. Indeed, all believers have been made priests unto God. Every sphere of influence can be a holy temple and every act done in the name of Jesus can be a spiritual sacrifice, acceptable to God through Jesus Christ. *Therefore, I beseech you brethren, by the mercies of God, that ye present your bodies in living sacrifice, holy, well pleasing unto God, which is your rational worship* (Romans 12:1).

# Chapter 8

# Avoiding the Tendency to Drift

Yes, it is *drifting* that is to be feared most. Men don't become atheists and swindlers with a single leap. For every person who decisively sets his face against God, there are hundreds who drift from Him.

In my own vacation experiences, an illustration occurred one time which taught me to fully evaluate the power of the tide to drift. We were staying on the coast of North Wales, and wanted to visit an island famous for its ruins and traditions. Nothing seemed easier than to cross the narrow straits which lay between it and the beach on which we stood. But as soon as our rowboat crossed beyond the jutting headland, we found ourselves caught by a strong current which persistently carried us off course, and if we had yielded to it, it would have carried us adrift far down the coast. It took four of us rowing hard for four and a half hours to cross the straits. Later that night, with a flowing tide, we traversed the same span in about half an hour.

Ever since that experience, I've never ignored the power of the current, so gentle, so imperceptible, so pleasant to yield to, and yet so difficult to resist. And I have often been reminded of that episode when I've seen young men drifting before the currents of moral influence on the great ocean of life.

Young men come up to our big cities from holy and blessed homes where they have been born and raised. They are nice, amiable, well-meaning fellows, with no intention of going wrong, though perhaps without a strong resolution to go right. The last words of advice from father or mother ring in their ears, urging them to keep up the good habits in which they have been trained since childhood, and they intend to conform to them.

If they fall in with a strong Christian influence, it isn't unlikely that they will turn out well enough. But if they go into some establishment or house where there is a fast set, merry with liquor, where the Lord's Day is unkept, where filthy insinuations pollute the talk, and gambling fills the leisure hours, after the first shock wears off, they give themselves up to the strong, prevailing current and begin to inertly but swiftly drift. At first, it isn't necessary that they commit some flagrant sin; it is enough that *they cease to resist* the insidious influences around them.

Young men, does this offer a true depiction of your condition? If so, be mindful of the advice of an elder brother who has passed through city life and can gather up all the advice he has in the words, *Don't drift.*

**Don't Drift into a Loose Way of Keeping Sunday**

When you are away from home, you don't know where to go, what church to attend, or what minister to listen to. If you enter a place of worship, no one knows you, and perhaps no one welcomes you. You miss the familiar faces and voices of your childhood's earliest memories. You feel your absence from that congregation and really from any other, and yet, you know your absence won't be noticed for the rest of the day and so you stay away. Your pursuits may be quite innocent, and yet your absence from God's house and neglect of your old practice, without sufficient reason, is the first symptom of yielding to the swift current which urges you to drift.

When relocating to a new place, my advice is to go to several different places of worship in the neighborhoods near where you live. Go once or twice to ascertain the character of the ministry and of the work carried on, and then join the one you find most helpful. Make direct contact with the minister, tell him who you are, where you have come from, and your intention of settling down in his congregation. If he is a true man of God, he will be only too glad to welcome you. If he isn't, I would advise you to take yourself to someone who will happily welcome you into the flock.

When you settle in a new place, be sure to surround yourself with good, Christian friends and some older gentlemen who may disciple you and offer spiritual support when difficult challenges come.

### Don't Drift into Loose Companionships

A man is made or tainted by his friends. In the same way a fish takes on the mottling of the ground on which it lies, and like the butterflies resemble the flowers over which they hover, so we become like those whom we choose for our companions. Don't drift into an acquaintance with any man until you are pretty sure of him and have asked God to show you his true character. *Be not deceived: evil companions corrupt good character* (1 Corinthians 15:33).

Beware of the man who goes in for a lot of showy jewelry and professes to be able to show you a thing or two about life. Perhaps he knows a little too much and wants to see life at your expense. And when you have spent your last penny and he is tired of you, he will hurl you aside without mercy.

Beware of the man who commonly belittles his mother, father, home, or women. Many men ridicule any hint of the purity and kindheartedness of those who make up the home, and apparently don't accept that woman can be anything other than the toy or victim of man. It is most likely that they have only lived to tempt the weaker sex whom they now criticize, and that their vices have essentially excluded them from the company of pure and virtuous women.

Beware of the man who professes to be too knowledgeable in the science of the day to believe in the Bible, and who ridicules those who do. It is an easy thing to ask a question which might take days of teaching and investigation to answer. Destructive criticism is child's play. Any fool can light a cathedral on fire, which would take centuries to rebuild; and any raggedly dressed homeless child wandering the streets can smash a window which neither modern wealth nor art can reconstruct. True wisdom is not destructive but constructive. A man has no more right to steal away or spoil your faith than he has to deprive you of your eyesight or rob you of your purse. And if he attempts it, he divulges a dangerous character of which it is best for you to be wary.

### Don't Drift into Extravagant Spending

It's better to live on oatmeal porridge and brown bread than spend more than you can afford and drift into debt. The pleasure of a day's outing or of an evening's fun has a nasty aftertaste when you have to avoid certain people for weeks or months because you owe them money that you can't repay.

We might be tempted to imitate people above us socially, but it's a miserable life to live and very unsatisfactory because we generally imitate their weaknesses and vices rather than their virtues. And yet it seems to offer much passing pleasure for the poor clerk to dress and speak with the airs of a young lord. One evening's conquest of the barmaids and bar loafers must be a rare luxury. But this kind of thing can't be done without money. You don't have much money to throw away out of ten dollars per week. The result is that a young man sometimes spends in a single evening

> It's better to live on oatmeal porridge and brown bread than spend more than you can afford and drift into debt.

enough money to fill his heart with anxiety for many a weary day; and in hope of the opportunity of repayment, which never comes, he may even be tempted to take money which doesn't belong to him in order to delay pressing demands.

## Don't Drift into Habits of Gambling

Plenty of gambling is all around us, and a man feels rather lonely when he refuses to join in. Some time ago I felt like this while onboard an ocean steamer, when I seemed to be nearly the only one who refused to join in a sweepstakes. Workshops and businesses not filled with the buzz of excitement on the eve of some great race are comparatively rare. And in most large towns, clubs and other similar places offer men the opportunity of losing fortunes, if they are only fools enough.

For the most part, it's not the love of money that urges men to bet, but the excitement of the chance – the risk – which relieves the monotony of their otherwise aimless existence. As we look on such people from outside, we can't conceive of the fascinations this kind of life offers, just as we can't truly comprehend the irresistible force of the whirlpool until we are being sucked into its gurgling vortex. But it is certainly needless to fling ourselves into them to see what they are like. Once pulled in, we will probably find it impossible to get out. And we can almost imperceptibly be drawn in. To deposit the first coin in a raffle or sweepstakes, to bet the first shilling on a horse, to lay a bet for a pair of gloves – these things may seem like nothing, but they are a form of yielding to the outer rim of the whirlpool.

Of course, it's easy to break from them, but they can lead to other things only a single hairbreadth removed from them, but which will lead to others, and still others beyond. How much better to put your foot down and refuse to take part in the first place. You intend to refuse to participate in the second, but if you are going to refuse at all, it will be unspeakably easier to refuse in the beginning than after you have taken part.

Betting is a bad thing. It undoes society in the same way the social white ant feeds on wood and is highly destructive to the wooden houses of the tropics. Men who bet care about little else. Love and home are sacrificed to the companions of the betting ring. Business is neglected because they live in the feverish hope of coming into a windfall and getting money without giving an equivalent of any sort.

### Don't Drift into Habits of Drinking

Nothing is easier to do than this. The tides of strong drink are running swiftly through our streets, and every corner saloon is a jetty from which men may enter the boats and launch upon the current. A few may enter it and still escape, but for an enormous number there is little hope of escape once they are somewhat afloat on the fascinating but perilous waters.

They say that smoking leads to drinking. Some of us have so many natural appetites to keep in order that we are thankful never to have awakened the habit of smoking, which seems a very masterful one and terribly able to become a tyrant and a very unhealthy one at that.

You aren't a sinner specifically because you smoke,

but is it wise to begin a habit you can't defend except by saying that others do it and besides being very unhealthy, may lead you into drinking, bad friendships, and other things?

But other things also cause a person to drift into drinking habits. Loafing about the streets in the evenings; paying the cost to treat your companions to a drink because you want to look significant in their regard and with the certainty that you will have to drink what they provide in return; doing business over a wine bar; spending your evenings in places like music halls, where alcohol passes around, and where the proprietor looks warily on those who don't patronize the buffet – all these are easy methods of drifting into drink.

No one plans to be a drunkard when he starts drinking. Those who are now in the agony of delirium were once as pure and true as you, but they were carried down an almost imperceptible slope. Beware of their fate, and don't follow their earlier steps, for fear you will gain momentum you can't halt and go down to hell. There is no better safeguard to a young man in life than to take the pledge of total abstinence. He may not sign a pledge at a meeting, but he can write one in his own bedroom and make up his mind that by God's help he will never touch this detestable enemy of human hearts, happiness, and homes.

### Don't Drift into Habits of Impurity

We all have appetites and desires within us that are beautiful and innocent enough when kept in their right place; but they are very reluctant to be kept there, and are always scraping to ascend the throne of control and to assume dominion over our life. It seems pleasant to allow them to ascend like this, but who will describe the horrors of the wreckage of all that is bright and beautiful and happy in the life of the miserable victim who has yielded to their first suggestions?

Beware of drifting into secret sins, witnessed by no eye but God's. Beware of keeping the company of those who are familiar with the ways of darkness and impurity. Beware of shows and pictures, of amusements and books that excite the lower passions. Never go to a place to which you could not take your mother or sister. Never get familiar with a girl whom you could not introduce to the purest woman you know. Never treat a girl in any way other than you would like a man to treat your own sister.

> **Beware of drifting into secret sins, witnessed by no eye but God's.**

It isn't necessary to yield to temptation. Abstinence from strong drink and excessive meat; plenty of gymnastics, cycling, and muscular exercise; hard mattresses, cold bathing, and *early* rising will remedy many of the issues which so often perplex young men. And better than all this is the power and purity of Jesus, which you can claim and use every time you need it. One sincere, believing cry for help will bring Him near. And when He enters the soul, impurity cannot stand against His indwelling any more than straw before fire or darkness before day.

### Don't Drift into an Imprudent Marriage

It is good when a young man meets a good girl. I never object to an early engagement when the couple are well mated, though I would urge a deferred marriage until the comforts of a home can be provided either by the love of friends or by the results of united savings. And no home is so sweet as that which has been chosen and furnished by the taste and self-denial of those who are to enter it.

You should not choose your life partner only from seeing her in an evening dress or in a group. Every sweet face doesn't tell a perfectly true story of the inner disposition. You need a wife who knows something more than how to play one or two set pieces on the piano, or how to sing half a dozen songs. The girl who understands all the details of household management, who knows how everything should be done even though she may never have to do it, who has been good to her parents and younger brothers and sisters, who dresses simply and neatly, who knows how to make a dollar and do a dollar's work, who is deeply spiritual – that is the kind of woman who will make a good wife. Until God sends her to you, don't flirt or play with a girl's affections, or lead any to think you care for them when you don't.

### Don't Drift into Being a Mere Moneymaking Machine

Some people seem to live for nothing other than to add a few more coins to their rising pile, and to do this, they sacrifice all that makes life sweet and decent and honorable. Have an aim high in character. Spend your life aiming for the best results. Be more eager to get *up* than to get *on*. There's no harm in ambition when it is directed toward doing the best you can to make the world better and those around you happier. But to seek money for money's sake is a detestable passion. Your aim must be to seek first the things that make for righteousness and peace, for God's glory and man's good. Be faithful in these, in your small sphere of influence, and it will be almost certain that you will be put in a position where you will have the chance of being also faithful in much. *But seek ye first the kingdom of God and his righteousness, and all these things shall be added unto you* (Matthew 6:33).

You tell me that you can't resist the strong current on which you are already launched, and that you have already started to drift. But it isn't too late. Send up a cry of distress to the Lord Jesus and ask Him to come on board your boat. He is stronger than the mightiest current. Give Him the towing line, so He can take it in His hand and tow you up the strong stream to His own bright home.

There is no better policy, dear young brother, than to give your heart to Jesus. Take Him as your Savior, Master, and Friend. Ask Him to live in your soul, making you pure and sweet and strong. Follow Him in His footsteps of self-sacrifice for the sake of others. Go no place where you can't also take Him. Let His friends be yours, and see that yours are His. Ask Him to put you into that position where you can please and glorify Him best. Remember that prayer and waiting will untie the toughest knots and unravel the greatest difficulties.

# Chapter 9

# A Few Words for Christian Girls

Dear friends,

I have many things to say to you (suggested by the experiences of our own church life and Bible classes), which I want you to think over quietly, so I will put them all into a letter you can keep and read again and again. As you read it, try to think of me as an elder brother who is eager to help you.

In all this world, there is nothing lovelier than the young life God has given you with its sunny laughter, its high spirits, its hopes and golden dreams, its wealth of pure love. You can enrich the poorest home like no money could. You can lighten the hardest lot in life. You can bring cheerfulness to the roughest path, making weary feet forget the sharp stones along the way. You can find the blue flowers blooming amid arctic snows, and by doing so, you may give and get untold blessings.

I am glad you've given your heart and life to the Lord Jesus. You will never regret that step by which Jesus has become your Brother. Remember how He said, *For whosoever doeth the will of God, the same is my . . . sister"* (Mark 3:35). And no one knows better than He does how much the tie between a strong and noble Brother and the sisters who shelter beneath His care means. He grew up with sisters in that village home under the blue Syrian skies; and, as the shadows of death gathered around His path, He made much of the love of His adopted sisters, Mary and Martha, in the home in Bethany.

Words fail me to tell you all that the Lord Jesus will do for you. He will keep your heart whiter than snow, removing each stain of sin by His own precious blood. He will put Himself as a shield between you and all types of hurt. He will make you His special responsibility and will quench your thirst from the brimming chalice of His own love. He will guide you through confusion, protect you in dangers, and supply all your need in times of necessity. He will give you what all women long for – the sense of belonging to someone good enough, wise enough, and strong enough, someone to trust without misgivings or fear.

But I hope you will be ALL for Him. This is the only path on which the sunbeams always play. There are many professing Christians who have just enough religion to make them miserable, and by their actions, they might as well be without any. They take a good drink of the sweets of the world and then try to quiet their conscience by a pilgrimage to the living well. But even though they rattle the chains and let down their buckets, they never get one pure crystal drop for their poor parched lips because they don't seek the Lord with *all* their heart. And so, after a little while, they rush off again to the gilded pleasures of the world.

Don't make their mistake. In the same way Jesus gave all for you, give all to Him and He will give you back one hundredfold. When you are unswervingly right with Christ, other things will right themselves.

### Dress

Dress perplexes some and takes up much time and thought. It is a difficult subject, and yet a Christian girl has several clear rules to guide her.

> Do not dress in a showy or extravagant manner or beyond your means.

> Do not dress in such a way as to call attention to any part of your figure or to distort or alter it.

> Do not dress so people will notice your dress more than you.

There is no reason why the general style of your dress shouldn't be like that of other people, because to be totally out of fashion would make you needlessly stand out and attract as much attention as if you were dressed to the height of fashion. And whatever makes others focus on us, or us think about ourselves, actually turns thoughts away from Jesus and from better things. I think there is no higher virtuosity for a Christian girl than to dress simply, quietly, and tastefully, as one who is careful about the body which Christ has given her, but who is also mindful of the apostle Paul's words: *In like manner also that the women adorn themselves in an honest manner, with shyness and modesty, not with ostentatious hair or gold or pearls or costly clothing* (1 Timothy 2:9).

## Ornaments

The use of ornaments is also a heart matter. It isn't a critical matter and is something to be settled between you and Christ. If you experience doubts, the little trinkets should be laid aside until the great Owner tells His servants what He would like them to do.

It does seem strange that so much money would be locked up in articles of personal adornment when the Lord's cause is suffering for lack of help. A Chinese Christian lady brought her jewels one morning to her husband, to build an Opium refuge, and when he expressed surprise, she said, "I have taken Christ for my adornment, and surely that is enough for any Christian woman."

**Put on the Lord Jesus, dear sisters, and you will lose your taste for many things you now hold dear.**

Put on the Lord Jesus, dear sisters, and you will lose your taste for many things you now hold dear, in the same way most girls would throw away glass jewelry if offered real gems. *Let their adorning not be outward with ostentatious hairdos and wearing of gold nor in composition of apparel, but let the interior adorning of the heart be without corruption, and of an agreeable spirit and peaceful, which is precious in the sight of God* (1 Peter 3:3-4).

The woman who loads herself with jewels confesses herself to be lacking in the jewels of the heart; but she who has obtained these, worries little about the diamonds or pearls of earthly mines.

## Amusements

Amusements also employ the time of many. We must have rest and change in these busy impetuous times, but we must watch our leisure hours so as not to let them do us more harm than good. Some ways of spending this free time simply increase the exhaustion of the jaded mind and tired body and make us unfit for quiet prayer or daily work.

For these reasons and others, you must keep clear of the theater, the concert hall, and the dancing saloon. You can't go to these places and keep the fullness of the Spirit or the love of Jesus. You can't go to them without hearing or seeing things which should bring a blush to the face. You can't go to them without putting yourself into the path of men with whom you should have no dealings whatsoever.

The atmosphere of such places will stain the best life, as gas blights tender plants. If you live near Christ, you will soon stop going to them, just like people put out their fires when the summer sun is shining. Remember the responsibilities and demands of home, the necessity for older sisters to throw themselves into the amusements of younger children, the many social and educational meetings held at churches and chapels, and other Christian institutions, and I am sure you will find there's no need for you to seek pleasure in things which leave a sting behind.

## Dancing

Dancing is a matter to be settled between you and Christ.

I have often wondered how girls who have any self-respect can yield themselves, especially when attired in the flimsy costume of a ballroom, to the embrace of strange men, whose morals may be worse than doubtful. It doesn't seem fitting that the body of a Christian, meant to be the temple of the Holy Spirit, should be whirled through the maze of a waltz by one whose linen may be spotless, but whose soul is dark with the ruin of some of your sisters, who, though fallen now, were once "white as the beautiful snow."

Young men are rather cautious about the girls they love going to these promiscuous dances, and a straw shows the drift of the stream. No sensible man will choose his wife in a ballroom, nor a wise woman her husband. On the other hand, a young Christian girl told me the other day that since she gave this up for Christ, He had filled her with unspeakable joy.

## Novels

Beware of reading novels. Many a magnificent tree has been eaten through by minute insects, and many a promising character has been inwardly rotted by certain kinds of novels and novelettes, especially those issued in cheap weekly issues. Some young friends of mine, when once bitten by this fever, have done nothing but read trashy and sentimental stories. They will deprive themselves of food and sleep to read them, and as a result, a great change takes place. They are so absorbed with the joys and sorrows of imaginary people that they overlook relationships within their immediate circle. Their appetite is so satiated by sweets that they have no interest in the Bread of Life. They talk to you like a person living in a dreamland of unreality.

I plead with you to guard against the insidious growth of this appetite. If you find it encroaching on you, break it off. Lay it aside in the strength of Christ, in the same way the runner lays aside every weight. *Leaving behind all the weight of the sin which surrounds us, let us run with patience the race that is set before us* (Hebrews 12:1). If you must read stories, read only those by the cleanest storytellers. Remember that there are many books about travel, history, and biography equal in interest to any fiction that was ever spun in the brain of man or woman.

> It is of the highest importance to keep absolutely pure.

### Purity

It is of the highest importance to keep absolutely pure. All around you are impure books, and men, and works – all ready to soil you, like the soot of ashes does to clean linen hung out to dry in some poor courtyard.

You must guard against their approach right from the start. Many a young girl has dated her ruin from her first smile at an indecent suggestion. The other day I heard about a married woman who said, as a young girl entered the workroom for the first time, "Let her sit by me; I will soon shock her." Shame on her! Regrettably, how much of this is going on everywhere. But, so long as you are pure, you will find that Christlike chastity is an armor from which all these poisoned darts will glance aside. Depend on it, that a woman can pass unhurt through the foulest environment if only her heart is pure and she is living in touch with Christ. Many times she will be able to frown down some indecent and unseemly joke or guard some young life.

### Marriage

In the same way Ruth did, every woman looks forward to being settled in the home of her husband. Unfortunately, in many cases, the woman finds herself dealing with disenchantment. The shores of time are strewn with the wrecks of women's loves and hopes, and all because they have forgotten that true human love must be grounded on the love and choice and will of God. Human love can't satisfy apart from the love of God.

Make Jesus your counsellor regarding your future.

And now, as I say farewell, please accept my sincerest wishes for your happiness in this world and the next. Be ready for the Bridegroom's coming and see that the lamp of your love is well supplied with the precious oil of the Holy Spirit, so you may be ready to go in at once to the marriage feast.

Your sincere friend and brother,

F. B. Meyer

# Chapter 10

# Seven Rules for Daily Living

These brief and simple words are intended for the many sincere Christians who are dissatisfied with their present life and long to enter that more blessed state of rest and peace of which they catch occasional glimpses, like white-plumaged seabirds that flash into view for a moment, far away over the breakers and then are lost to sight.

Now from my own experience I suggest these seven rules to live by to my fellow Christians:

## 1. Make a Definite Consecration of Yourselves to God

In his diary, Dr. Doddridge has left a very beautiful form of self-consecration. With most it would be sufficient to write out Miss Havergal's hymn, "Take My Life and Let It Be," and to sign their names at the bottom of the page.

Take my life and let it be
Consecrated, Lord, to Thee.

Take my hands and let them move
At the impulse of Thy love.

Take my feet and let them be
Swift and beautiful for Thee.

Take my voice and let me sing
Always, only, for my King.

Take my lips and let them be
Filled with messages from Thee.

Take my silver and my gold,
Not a mite would I withhold.

Take my moments and my days,
Let them flow in endless praise.

Take my intellect and use
Every pow'r as Thou shalt choose.

Take my will and make it Thine,
It shall be no longer mine.

Take my heart, it is Thine own,
It shall be Thy royal throne.

Take my love, my God, I pour
At Thy feet its treasure store.

Take myself, and I will be
Ever, only, all for Thee.

In any case, it is best to write down some record of

your new birth, to keep for future reference. Of course, it's worth saying, when we have really given ourselves once, we cannot give ourselves a second time, because Jesus said, *I give unto them eternal life; and they shall never perish, neither shall anyone pluck them out of my hand. My Father, who gave them to me, is greater than all; and no one is able to pluck them out of my Father's hand* (John 10:28-29). We can renew the consecration vows; we can review the deed of gift;[8] we can insert any new clauses we like; and if we have gone astray, we can ask the Lord to forgive the dishonest wrong and robbery we have done Him, and to restore our souls into the position from which we have fallen. Oh, how sweet the promise, *He restores my soul* (Psalm 23:3). Dear Christian reader, seek some quiet spot, some tranquil time, and yield yourself to God.

## 2. Tell God You Are Willing to Be Made Willing in All Ways

A lady once faced great difficulties regarding certain things which she felt eager to keep under her own control. Her friend who wished to urge her into the better life of consecration, placed before her a blank sheet of paper, and pressed her to write her name at the bottom, and then to lay it before God in prayer. She did so, and instantly entered this blessed Christian life.

Are you willing to do this? Are you prepared to sign your name to a blank sheet of paper and then hand it over to God for Him to fill in as He pleases? If not,

---

8    A legal agreement to give property to someone without charging them any money.

ask Him to make you willing and able to do this and everything else. You will never be happy until you let the Lord Jesus keep the house of your nature, closely scrutinizing every visitor and admitting only His friends. He must reign. He must have all or nothing. He must have the key of every closet, of every cupboard, and of every room. Do not try to make them fit for Him. Simply give Him the key. He will cleanse and renovate and make beautiful.

### 3. Count on Christ to Do His Part Perfectly

As soon as you give, He takes. You open the door and He immediately enters. You roll back the floodgates, and He pours in a glorious tide of fullness – fullness of wealth, power, and joy. The clay only has to be formed by the hand of a Palissy.[9] The marble only has to be workable to the chisel of a Michelangelo. The organ only has to be responsive to the slightest touch of a Handel. The student only has to follow the slightest hint of a Faraday or a Whewell, and there will be no failure in results. Oh, to be equally swayable to the molding influences of Christ. If we will just let Him do His work unhindered, we will not fail in realizing the highest ideal of which we are capable.

> Simply give Him the key. He will cleanse and renovate and make beautiful.

---

9    Palissy ware is a nineteenth-century term for ceramics produced in the style of the famous French potter Bernard Palissy (1510–1590).

### 4. Confess Sin Instantly

If you allow acid to drop and remain on your steel fenders, it will corrode them, and if you allow sin to remain on your heart unconfessed, it will eat out all peace and rest.

Don't wait for evening to come or until you can get alone, but *there* in the midst of the crowd, in the very rush of life, with the footprints of sin still fresh, lift up your heart to your merciful and ever-present Savior, and say, "Lord Jesus, wash me now from that sin in Your precious blood, and I shall be whiter than snow." *Remove the sin in me . . . and I shall be clean; wash me, and I shall be whiter than snow* (Psalm 51:7). The blood of Jesus is always at work, cleansing us from unconscious sin, but it is our part to request it be applied to cleanse us from conscious and known sins as soon as we are aware of their presence in our lives.

### 5. Hand Over Every Temptation and Care to Christ

When you feel temptation approaching you, like a bird is aware that the hawk is hovering near by some quick instinct, then instantly lift your heart to Christ for deliverance. He cannot reject or fail you. *He shall cover thee with his feathers, and under his wings thou shalt be secure* (Psalm 91:4). And when any petty annoyance or heavier worry threatens to mar your peace, in the flash of a moment, hand it over to Jesus, saying, "Lord, I am oppressed; take this on for me."

"Ah!" you sigh, "I certainly wish I could live like this, but in the moment of need I forget to look." Then do this: trust in Christ to keep you trusting. Look to Him to abide in you so as to keep you abiding. In the early morning, entrust the keeping of your soul to Him, and then with each succeeding hour expect Him to keep that which you have committed to Him.

### 6. Keep in Touch with Christ

Avoid the spirit of faultfinding, criticism, uncharitableness, and anything else inconsistent with His perfect love. Go where He is most likely to be found, either where two or three of His children are gathered, or where the lost sheep is straying. Ask Him to wake you each morning for fellowship and Bible study. Set another time in the day, especially in the still hour of the evening twilight between the work of the day and the pursuits of the evening. When you get alone with Him, tell Him everything, and review the past under the gentle light which streams from His eyes.

### 7. Expect the Holy Spirit to Work in, with, and for You

When a man is right with God, God will freely use him. Within him, impulses, inspirations, strong determinations, and strange resolves will rise up. These must be tested by Scripture and prayer, and if clearly from God, they must be obeyed.

But there is this perennial source of comfort: God's commands are enabling. He will never give us a work to do without showing exactly how and when to do it, and without giving us the precise strength and wisdom we need. Don't dread to enter this new life because you fear God will ask you to do something you cannot do. He will never do that. If He lays anything on your heart, He will do so irresistibly, and as you pray about it, the impression will continue to grow, so that now, as you look up to know what He wills you to say or do, the way will suddenly open, and you will probably have said the word or done the deed almost unconsciously.

In this life, there may be failures, but they will arise on the human side, not the divine. It will be best if we can rapidly discover the cause of failure, confess it, and seek restoration to the old peace and joy. After all, the sheep doesn't keep the shepherd; the shepherd keeps the sheep, and feeds it, and leads it, and makes it to lie down. Can't we expect the same from our Good Shepherd? And who can paint the lushness of the green pastures, or the crystal beauty of those unfailing springs to which He will lead the submissive and trustful spirit?

May that spirit be yours, dear reader, and mine.

# F. B. Meyer –
# A Brief Biography

Frederick Brotherton Meyer (1847-1929) was a Bible teacher, pastor, and evangelist of German descent born in London. He attended Brighton College and graduated from the University of London in 1869. He studied theology at Regent's Park College, Oxford, and went on to serve the Lord as a Baptist pastor and evangelist in England. He also devoted time to inner-city mission work in England and in America.

Meyer first became a pastor in 1870 at Pembroke Baptist Chapel in Liverpool. By 1872, he had moved on to pastor at Priory Street Baptist Church in York. It was during his tenure there that he met the well-known American evangelist Dwight L. Moody. The two of them became good friends, and the Lord used him to introduce Moody to other churches in England.

From Pembroke, he went on to pastor a number of other churches. When he accepted the pastorate at Christ Church in Lambeth in 1892, he found a meager congregation of only 100 faithful people attending; but over the next two years, God used him to breathe new life into the church and blessed him with more than two thousand people attending on a regular basis. God planted him at Christ Church for the next seventeen years, and then sent him out to preach at conferences and evangelistic services. These evangelistic circuits included trips to South Africa and Asia, and even carried him across the Atlantic a number of times to the United States and Canada.

Meyer was known for his outcry against immorality and other social evils. He was part of the Higher Life Movement, which was devoted to scriptural and practical Christian holiness. As a result, he tirelessly championed for the poor and needy, and his life and message were responsible for closing down more than five hundred saloons and houses of prostitution. He also initiated a prison aid society. Higher Life conferences were held at Broadlands (1874), Oxford (1874), Brighton (1875), and finally at Keswick (1875). Keswick quickly became the center of the movement, which also became known as the Keswick Movement, and for many years, he was closely associated with the Keswick Conventions.

During one of these conventions in 1887, as he sat listening to Hudson Taylor of the China Inland Mission speak, he suddenly realized something was missing in his life. Hudson Taylor possessed something he did not – the baptism of the Holy Spirit. That evening he walked from the Keswick tent and up a nearby a hill. Later he said:

I was too tired to agonize, so I left the prayer meeting and as I walked I said, "My Father, if there is one soul more than another within the circle of these hills that needs the gift of Pentecost, it is I. I want the Holy Spirit, but I do not know how to receive Him and I am too weary to think, or feel, or pray intensively." Then a Voice said to me, "As you took forgiveness from the hand of the dying Christ, take the Holy Ghost from the hand of the living Christ and reckon that the gift is thine by a faith that is utterly indifferent to the presence or absence of resultant joy. According to thy faith so shall it be unto thee." So I turned to Christ and said, "Lord, as I breathe in this whiff of warm night air, so breathe into every part of me Thy blessed Spirit." I felt no hand laid on my head, there was no lambent flame, there was no rushing sound from heaven: but by faith without emotion, without excitement, I took, and took for the first time, and I have kept on taking ever since.[10]

This experience changed his life, and as an evangelical of singular vision, his obituary in *The Daily Telegraph* described him as "The Archbishop of the Free Churches." As an author, he sold five million copies of his books during his lifetime. In all, he penned more than forty books, including Christian biographies on the lives of Samuel, David, Paul, Moses, Abraham, and others, as well as devotional Bible commentaries written to help Christians in their daily walk with Christ. Meyer served as president of the Free Church Council (1904), president of the World's Sunday School

---

10    Robert T. Henry, *The Golden Age of Preaching: Men Who Moved the Masses* (Lincoln, NE: iUniverse, 2005), 191.

Association (1907), and president of the Baptist Union (1907). But with all these accomplishments, Meyer made it clear that all credit went to God. He said, "I am only an ordinary man. I have no special gifts. I am no orator, no scholar, no profound thinker. If I have done anything for Christ and my generation, it is because I have given myself entirely to Christ Jesus, and then tried to do whatever He wanted me to do."

Meyer influenced giants of the faith like Charles H. Spurgeon, who said, "Meyer preaches as a man who has seen God face to face." From 1904 to 1905, he served as president of the National Federation of Free Churches, and following that term, he served as an evangelist for that organization.

In his seventies, F. B. Meyer returned to the work of pastoring churches in England but still traveled to the United States and Canada. At the age of eighty, he crossed the Atlantic one last time for his twelfth American preaching campaign for the Lord with a preaching style characterized as simple and direct. This campaign involved traveling more than fifteen thousand miles and speaking at more than three hundred meetings.

He led a long and fruitful life, preaching more than sixteen thousand sermons before he went home to be with the Lord in 1929 at the age of eighty-two.

# Similar Updated Classics

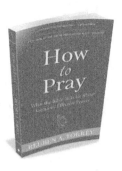

## How to Pray,
## by Reuben A. Torrey

Prayer. Satan laughs as he looks at the church today and says to himself, "You can have your Sunday schools and your young people's small groups, your boys' and girls' programs, your vacation Bible schools, your Christian schools, your elegant churches, your retreats, your music programs, your brilliant preachers, and even your revival efforts – as long as you don't bring the power of almighty God into them by earnest, persistent, believing, mighty prayer."

May God use this book to inspire many who are currently prayerless, or nearly so, to pray earnestly. May God stir up your own heart to be one of those burdened to pray, and to pray until God answers.

*Available where books are sold.*

## 5 Things Christians Must Do,
## by F. B. Meyer

This book is a refreshing, interesting, and yet challenging look at five essential aspects of healthy Christian living. These are not new, of course, as nothing can be added to what's been already recorded in scripture. Rather, the topics as they are written are a breath of fresh air in simplicity of presentation, yet striking to the core of what is necessary in order to truly follow Christ.

*Available where books are sold.*

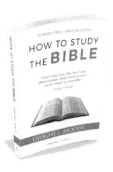

## *How to Study the Bible,*
## by Dwight L. Moody

There is no situation in life for which you cannot find some word of consolation in Scripture. If you are in affliction, if you are in adversity and trial, there is a promise for you. In joy and sorrow, in health and in sickness, in poverty and in riches, in every condition of life, God has a promise stored up in His Word for you.

This classic book by Dwight L. Moody brings to light the necessity of studying the Scriptures, presents methods which help stimulate excitement for the Scriptures, and offers tools to help you comprehend the difficult passages in the Scriptures. To live a victorious Christian life, you must read and understand what God is saying to you. Moody is a master of using stories to illustrate what he is saying, and you will be both inspired and convicted to pursue truth from the pages of God's Word.

*Available where books are sold.*

## *The Overcoming Life,* by Dwight L. Moody

Are you an overcomer? Or, are you plagued by little sins that easily beset you? Even worse, are you failing in your Christian walk, but refuse to admit and address it? No Christian can afford to dismiss the call to be an overcomer. The earthly cost is minor; the eternal reward is beyond measure.

Dwight L. Moody is a master at unearthing what ails us. He uses stories and humor to bring to light the essential principles of successful Christian living. Each aspect of overcoming is looked at from a practical and understandable angle. The solution Moody presents for our problems is not religion, rules, or other outward corrections. Instead, he takes us to the heart of the matter and prescribes biblical, God-given remedies for every Christian's life. Get ready to embrace genuine victory for today, and joy for eternity.

*Available where books are sold.*

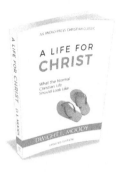

## *A Life for Christ*, by Dwight L. Moody

In the church today, we have everything buttoned up perfectly. The music is flawless, the sermon well-prepared and smoothly delivered, and the grounds meticulously kept. People come on time and go home on time. But a fundamental element is missing. The business of church has undermined the individual's need to truly live for Christ, so much so, that only a limited few are seeing their life impact the world.

Dwight L. Moody takes us deep into Scripture and paints a clear picture of what ought to be an individual's life for Christ. The call for each Christian is to become an active member in the body of Christ. The motive is love for the Lord and our neighbor. The result will be the salvation of men, women, and children everywhere.

*Available where books are sold.*

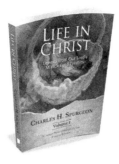

### *Life in Christ,* by Charles H. Spurgeon

Men who were led by the hand or groped their way along the wall to reach Jesus were touched by his finger and went home without a guide, rejoicing that Jesus Christ had opened their eyes. Jesus is still able to perform such miracles. And, with the power of the Holy Spirit, his Word will be expounded and we'll watch for the signs to follow, expecting to see them at once. Why shouldn't those who read this be blessed with the light of heaven? This is my heart's inmost desire.

*Available where books are sold.*